Tories, Terror, and Tea

True Stories of Pennsylvania &
Pennsylvanians in the
American Revolutionary War

JOHN L. MOORE

Mechanicsburg, PA USA

Published by Sunbury Press, Inc.
Mechanicsburg, Pennsylvania

www.sunburypress.com

Copyright © 2017 by John L. Moore.
Cover Copyright © 2017 by Sunbury Press, Inc.

Sunbury Press supports copyright. Copyright fuels creativity, encourages diverse voices, promotes free speech, and creates a vibrant culture. Thank you for buying an authorized edition of this book and for complying with copyright laws by not reproducing, scanning, or distributing any part of it in any form without permission. You are supporting writers and allowing Sunbury Press to continue to publish books for every reader. For information contact Sunbury Press, Inc., Subsidiary Rights Dept., PO Box 548, Boiling Springs, PA 17007 USA or legal@sunburypress.com.

For information about special discounts for bulk purchases, please contact Sunbury Press Orders Dept. at (855) 338-8359 or orders@sunburypress.com.

To request one of our authors for speaking engagements or book signings, please contact Sunbury Press Publicity Dept. at publicity@sunburypress.com.

ISBN: 978-1-62006-790-1 (Trade paperback)

Library of Congress Control Number: 2017934117

FIRST SUNBURY PRESS EDITION: March 2017

Product of the United States of America
0 1 1 2 3 5 8 13 21 34 55

Set in Bookman Old Style
Designed by Crystal Devine
Cover by Lawrence Knorr
Edited by Allyson Gard

Continue the Enlightenment!

Dedication

For Thomas J. Brucia, an old and valued friend whose advice, encouragement and criticism has made this a better book. Tom serves as both a writer's friend and a reader's advocate.

Cover Art: A sentry belonging to the 8th Pennsylvania Regiment on duty at Valley Forge during the winter of 1777-78. The scene is by traditional frontier artist Andrew Knez Jr.

Contents

Acknowledgments   vii

Author's Note   ix

CHAPTER ONE
*1773: How It Became Unpatriotic for
Americans to Drink Tea*   1

CHAPTER TWO
*1775: Frontiersmen March to Boston
to the Sound of Fifes, Drums*   5

CHAPTER THREE
*1776: 'I am afraid,' Loyalist Lawyer
Confides to his Journal*   16

CHAPTER FOUR
*1777: The 'Hair Buyer' Rewards
Indians Bringing Him Scalps*   28

CHAPTER FIVE
*1777: Congress Flees as British
Approach Philadelphia*   36

CHAPTER SIX
*1777: Pennsylvania Soldiers Have
Dire Need of Shoes, Shirts*   48

CHAPTER SEVEN
*1777: 'An Indian War Is Now Raging
Around Us in its Utmost Fury'*   58

CHAPTER EIGHT
*1778: Shortage of Lead Triggers
Severe Scarcity of Bullets* 68

CHAPTER NINE
*1778: Tories, War Parties Terrorize
Susquehanna Settlements* 76

CHAPTER TEN
*1778: Captured Settler Forced
to Live Like an Indian* 87

CHAPTER ELEVEN
*1782: Indians, British Rangers Burn
Frontier Town in Western Pa.* 95

CHAPTER TWELVE
*1782: 'Hijacker Pointed Pistol, Said
He'd Blow My Brains Out'* 100

Bibliography 111

About the Author 113

Acknowledgments

I am indebted to my wife, Jane E. Moore, as well as friends Thomas J. Brucia and Robert B. Swift for critiquing the manuscript and for suggesting improvements.

Author's Note on Quotations

I have taken a journalist's approach to writing about the people whose lives and experiences are chronicled in this book. Long dead, they nonetheless speak to us through the many letters, diaries, journals, official reports, depositions, interrogations, examinations, minutes, and memoirs that they left behind.

Whenever possible, I have presented the people I have written about in their own words. My intent is to allow the reader a sense of immediacy with historical figures who lived two or more centuries ago. To accomplish this, I have occasionally omitted phrases or sentences from quotations, and I have employed an ellipsis (. . .) to indicate where I have done so. In some instances, I have modernized punctuation; and in others, spelling has been modernized.

John L. Moore
Northumberland, PA
January 2017

CHAPTER ONE

1773

How It Became Unpatriotic for Americans to Drink Tea

Once a popular beverage in colonial Pennsylvania, tea rapidly lost favor after America's colonists learned in mid-1773 that the British government intended to tax it.

In Philadelphia, news of the tax plan prompted a political uproar. City residents gathered for an open public meeting on Oct. 18, declaring, "It is the duty of every American to oppose this attempt." The levy was denounced as "a tax on the Americans . . . without their consent."

Located along the Delaware River about 120 miles from the Atlantic Ocean, Philadelphia was a deep-water port. Residents quickly realized that an English merchant ship would soon bring a cargo of tea to their wharves.

Word arrived from England that in August 1773, the East India Company had decided to ship 600 chests of tea to Philadelphia aboard The Polly, a sailing ship with a cargo capacity of about 250 tons. A man named Ayres would be captain.

Port of Philadelphia in the 1700s

This news infuriated the Pennsylvanians, who organized an entity called The Committee for Tarring and Feathering. On Nov. 27 the committee published a handbill urging the port's river pilots—men who guided ocean-going vessels up the Delaware to Philadelphia—to watch for The Polly.

A "handsome reward" might well go to the waterman first to spot the tea ship, "but all agree that tar and feathers will be his portion who pilots her into this harbor," said the handbill, which was signed by such fictional notables as Thomas Tarbuckett, Peter Pitch and Benjamin Brush.

The committee also threatened to tar and feather The Polly's captain himself—Captain Ayres.

Meanwhile, the East India Company was sending tea shipments to other colonial ports. In Boston, for instance, the Sons of Liberty, dressed as Indians, dumped the company's tea into the harbor on December 16 rather than allow it to be brought ashore and to be taxed.

It was late in 1773 when word reached Philadelphia that The Polly had sailed into the Delaware.

On Saturday, December 25, "an express came up from Chester to inform the town that the tea ship commanded by Captain Ayres, with her detested cargo, was arrived there, having followed another ship up the river," the *Pennsylvania Gazette* reported.

Events happened rapidly after that. In the morning of Sunday, December 26, a citizens committee created just to deal with the tea ship appointed three representatives to go to Chester, about 15 miles downriver, and to bring Ayres to Philadelphia. But when the three men reached Chester, The Polly had already weighed anchor and was sailing upriver.

As the ship passed Gloucester Point, about four miles south of the Philadelphia, other representatives of the citizens committee were waiting. "As she passed along, she was hailed, and the captain (was) requested not to proceed farther, but to come on shore. This the captain complied with," the *Pennsylvania Gazette* reported.

Ayres agreed to go to Philadelphia. The tea committee convened a public meeting to decide what should be done with The Polly's cargo. So many people turned out that the committee held the meeting out of doors in the public square across from the State House, now known as Independence Hall.

The captain, quickly sensing the temper of the citizens, readily agreed that The Polly wouldn't attempt to land. Instead, he permitted a river pilot take his ship to Reedy Island, about 55 miles downriver. Ayres himself stayed in Philadelphia long enough to obtain supplies his crew needed for the return trip to London.

As the *Pennsylvania Journal* reported in its December 29 edition: "Yesterday at three quarters of an hour after 2 o'clock, Captain Ayres . . . left Arch Street wharf on board a pilot boat, (having been 46 hours in town,) to follow the ship to Reedy Island, and from thence transport the East India Company's (tea) to . . . London. He was attended to the wharf by a concourse of people, who wished him a good voyage."

As a beverage, coffee surged in popularity after that. Indeed, it became a patriotic act to drink a cup of java.

CHAPTER TWO

1775

Frontiersmen March to Boston to the Sound of Fifes, Drums

Traveling on horseback, a 27-year-old Presbyterian preacher named Philip Vickers Fithian rode circuits during the spring and summer of 1775 through the back country of Virginia and Pennsylvania. The fighting at Lexington and at Concord had happened in faraway Massachusetts during April, but everywhere Fithian went, he found frontiersmen putting themselves on a footing for war.

Stopping in the Shenandoah Valley to preach at the northern Virginia village of Stephensburg (present-day Stephens City), Fithian tarried for a week. At 4 o'clock in the afternoon of Monday, June 5, he saw "men busy mustering." The women of the village

Philip Vickers Fithian

were "in the street, and at doors, looking on." His journal entry for Tuesday, June 6, noted: "The drum beats, and the inhabitants of this village muster each morning at five o'clock."

The militia captain at Stephensburg was a "Mr. Holmes," with whom Fithian lodged. "He declares himself willing to leave his family, his store, and, on the first demand, march to the relief of any part of America," Fithian wrote on Saturday, June 3. "Here every presence is warlike, every sound is martial! Drums beating, fifes and bag-pipes playing, and . . . every man has a hunting-shirt, which is the uniform of each company. Almost all have a cockade, and bucks tail in their hats, to represent that they are hardy, resolute, and invincible natives of the woods."

Friday, June 23, found Fithian on horseback, well north of the Shenandoah Valley, riding alone through a narrow Pennsylvania valley. He was headed for Northumberland, a new town in the forks of the Susquehanna River where the Presbytery had scheduled him to preach on Sunday, July 1. Horse and rider spent much of the day on the trail, progressing slowly north along "a most stony valley, two high mountains on every side, the passage so narrow that you may take one stone in your right hand, and another in your left, and throw each upon a mountain."

The trail itself "was only a small footpath, and covered all with small sharp stones," he wrote. It rained all day, and he and his horse couldn't help but brush against the wet leaves from the trees and bushes that closed in upon the path. They were "all through besoaked" when they reached the residence of James Gray "in a little hamlet in the woods."

Gray and his family lived in present-day Juniata County, about 15 miles south of the Juniata River, which Fithian crossed near Mifflintown, then called Cedar Spring, the next day.

The farmer welcomed the traveler, provided "good pasture for my horse," and agreed to accommodate Fithian with both an evening meal and a place to stay for the night. "His good wife prepared me a warm, suitable supper," the preacher wrote in his journal.

But even here, deep in the Pennsylvania woods, Fithian couldn't get away from thoughts of politics and war: "Forgive me, my country," he wrote. "I supped on tea! It relieved me, however, and I went soon to bed."

By June 28 the preacher was in Northumberland, a village of log houses, when a company of soldiers came in from upriver settlements along the Susquehanna's West Branch. "About 12 o'clock marched into this town, from the Great Island, or Indian land, 50 miles up the river (at modern Lock Haven), 30 young fellows, all expert riflemen, with a drum and fife, under Captain Lowdon," Fithian wrote. Bound for Boston, which a British army had occupied, the frontiersmen were walking to Massachusetts—nearly 400 miles away—where they intended to join the American army. Along the way, they were stopping in towns and villages long enough to recruit additional men. "They passed on, however, soon to Sunbury, where they remained until Monday," Fithian wrote.

The men that Fithian encountered in Northumberland had come down the West Branch in response to a call from the Continental Congress, meeting in Philadelphia that June. With armed conflict under way at Boston, the Congress had asked Pennsylvania and two other colonies—Maryland and Virginia—to raise companies of independent riflemen. When organized, these soldiers "shall march and join the (American) army near Boston," the Congress said.

As John Adams, then a congressional delegate from Massachusetts, reported in a June 17, 1775, letter, the Congress had voted to send "10 companies of riflemen . . . from Pennsylvania, Maryland and Virginia, to join the army before Boston. These are an excellent species of light infantry, . . . the most accurate marksmen in the world." Adams said that their key weapon was "a peculiar kind" of firearm—"a rifle." The weapon has "circular . . . grooves within the barrel, and carries a ball, with great exactness to great distances."

One of the riflemen who joined at Northumberland was Private Aaron Wright, who kept a journal in which he recorded the experiences that he and his comrades had as they marched from Northumberland to Boston. Their captain was John Lowdon, who had settled near Mifflinburg in present-day Union County in 1772. In Northumberland on June 29, "we were sworn to be true and faithful soldiers in the Continental Army."

The riflemen crossed the North Branch and camped in Sunbury through July 7, "when we got orders to march," Private Wright wrote: ". . .

The next morning we marched on board the boats with as good spirits as ever men did."

The boats took them 60 miles downriver past Harris's Ferry (present-day Harrisburg), most likely to Middletown, a growing port at the mouth of the Swatara Creek. Here the soldiers disembarked and resumed their march. On July 13, "we reached Reading, where we got our regimentals, knapsacks and blankets," Wright reported. ("Regimentals" were uniforms worn by the men of a specific regiment.)

At Reading, they rendezvoused with other rifle companies also headed to Massachusetts. The daily accounts kept by some of these soldiers reflect the tedious and wearying nature of their trek to Boston, some 350 miles to the northeast. "Here we met Captains Patterson, Smith, Lowden, and Nagle, with their companies, destined for Cambridge," reported Captain William Hendricks, who reached Reading after a four-day march from Carlisle "with my company of 90 men." Rather than leave her in Pennsylvania, one of Hendricks' sergeants, Joseph Greer, had taken his wife along on the journey.

Accompanied by the rifle company of Captain John Chambers, Hendricks and his men left Carlisle on Thursday, July 13. "First day came to John Harris's ferry on Susquehanna River, two miles wide, and there we encamped." It took them another four days to reach Reading, a town only 60 miles to the east. They "stayed at Reading until the 22nd," the captain said.

These ranger-style soldiers were intentionally dressed in the style of Indian warriors.

"Each man," said John J. Henry, a Lancaster rifleman in Smith's Company. ". . . bore a rifle-barreled gun, a tomahawk, or small axe, and a long knife, usually called a scalping-knife, which served for all purposes in the woods. His underdress, by no means in a military style, was covered by a deep ash-colored hunting-shirt, leggings and moccasins, if the latter could be procured."

In early August, a Philadelphian received a letter from a friend in Frederick, Maryland, who told of "seeing Captain Michael Cresap marching at the head of a formidable company of perhaps one hundred and thirty men, from the mountains and backwoods, painted like Indians, armed with tomahawks and rifles, dressed in hunting shirts and moccasins . . ."

As the Marylanders moved out of the western mountains and passed through settled regions, they sometimes treated the townspeople to shooting exhibitions. At Lancaster, Pennsylvania, for example, "two brothers in the company took a piece of board five inches broad and seven inches long, with a bit of white paper, about the size of a dollar, nailed in the center, and while one of them supported this board perpendicularly between his knees, the other, at the distance of upwards of sixty yards, and without any kind of rest, shot eight bullets through it successively, and spared a brother's thigh," the *Pennsylvania Journal* reported in its August 23 edition.

A story that the *Virginia Gazette* ran on July 22 said that a recruiting officer for a Pennsylvania company had more volunteers than he could accommodate. To identify the best marksmen, he tested their skill: "He, with a piece of chalk, drew on a board the figure of a nose of the common size, which he placed at the distance of one hundred and fifty yards, declaring that those who should come nearest the mark should be enlisted. Sixty odd hit the object." The newspaper article ended with a warning to General Thomas Gage, the British commander at Boston. "General Gage," it cautioned, "take care of your nose."

Hendricks' company crossed the Delaware River into New Jersey on Friday, August 25; the riflemen then headed northeast towards the Hudson River.

As 1775 progressed, the Americans came to regard the professional army that Britain had sent to Boston from Britain as representing the ministers of the British government rather than King George III. The redcoats were often spoken of as "ministerial troops." ". . . For we do not, nor cannot yet prevail upon ourselves to call them the king's troops," George Washington explained in a May 31 letter written in Philadelphia.

In this vein, loyalists who actively challenged men who had taken up arms against the British became derided as "ministerial tools." As the riflemen crossed northern New Jersey on Saturday the 26th, they encountered a Tory with whom they had a dispute. As Captain Hendricks wrote, ". . . We tarred and feathered one of the ministerial tools, who refused to comply with the resolves of our Continental Congress."

By Sunday, July 30, Hendricks's troops arrived at New Windsor, New York, on the west shore on the "North or Hudson's river." They remained at New Windsor on Monday: "Rested . . . to get our linens washed, and ourselves recruited (refreshed), being weary, marching in exceeding hot weather," the captain wrote.

Aaron Wright's company took several weeks longer to reach the Hudson, and on August 26, the recruits crossed the Connecticut River near Hartford, Connecticut. As they marched, they soon learned that not every colonist wanted to rebel against George III. In the vicinity of Hartford, Wright and his comrades encountered a man who identified himself as Joseph Brooks. Brooks made the mistake of "saying he was sorry to see so many men going to fight the king." Clearly the man was a Tory, and the soldiers "took him two miles and tarred and feathered him."

Some weeks earlier, another company of riflemen had also endured the insults of an outspoken loyalist as they crossed Connecticut. That Tory called them "damned rebels." This happened at New Milford, north of Danbury. They responded by forcing him to walk with them as they marched to Litchfield. For good measure, the riflemen made the man carry a goose for the entire distance of 19 miles. "When they arrived there, they tarred him, and made him pluck his goose, and then bestowed the feathers on him," according to Barber's Historical Collections of Connecticut.

It was early September when Captain Lowdon's company reached Boston. It joined the Rifle Battalion commanded by Colonel William Thompson of Carlisle, and thus became part of the Second Regiment of the Army of the United Colonies, commanded by General George Washington.

"They are remarkably stout and hardy men; many of them exceeding six feet in height," reported James Thacher, a surgeon in the Continental Army. "They are dressed in white frocks, or rifle shirts, and round hats. These men are remarkable for the accuracy of their aim; striking a mark with great certainty at two hundred yards distance."

The riflemen impressed the surgeon favorably: "At a review, a company of them, while on a quick advance, fired their balls into objects of seven inches diameter, at the distance of two hundred and fifty yards. They are now stationed on our lines, and their shot have frequently proved fatal to British officers and soldiers, who expose themselves to view, even at more than double the distance of common musket shot."

The company was soon stationed on Ploughed Hill (in present-day Somerville, Massachusetts) near Bunker Hill in Boston Harbor. The Continentals occasionally traded shots, usually cannon fire, with the British soldiers. On September 20, for instance, "the Red Coats fired eight bombs and four cannon at our people on Ploughed Hill, which did us no other hurt that kill one steer that was in a pasture 300 yards from Ploughed Hill," Wright said.

There was more of the same on October 5: "The (British) regulars below Roxbury fired 86 cannon at our people and killed two cows and shot the arm of a musket man who stood behind an apple tree," he said.

In early March 1776, the riflemen were sent south of Boston to Roxbury, where "our men were building forts" on a neck of land.

Howe and British Forces evacuating Boston, 1776

Around 8 p.m. on March 9, "the regulars began to cannonade us very smartly," Wright wrote on March 10. The firing "was continued all night, and was returned by four of our forts. We lost four men by one ball, and one by another, each of whom, at a moderate computation, cost the butchers 350 pounds of powder, besides balls, of which the Continental army gathered 900 today."

On some future day at some other place, the Americans no doubt fired many of these cannonballs back at the British, but by March 10, the fighting at Boston was pretty much over. Realizing that the Continentals had them bottled up, the British commanders called in the fleet and on March 17, 1776, evacuated Boston.

As the Revolution progressed, one of the riflemen recruited at Northumberland, Timothy Murphy, became a sniper of renown. In addition to taking part in the Siege of Boston, Murphy was credited with service at the battles of Long Island, Trenton and Princeton. Later he belonged to Colonel Daniel Morgan's corps of riflemen. Legend credits Murphy with firing a 300-yard shot that killed a British brigadier general, Simon Fraser, during the Second Battle of Saratoga in October 1777. Fraser's death contributed to the British surrender.

Historical fact places Timothy Murphy among the riflemen who accompanied Major General John Sullivan's expedition against the Iroquois Indians in the Finger Lakes region of New York in August and September 1779. Murphy survived the September 13 ambush near Conesus Lake that killed most of the soldiers on a patrol led by Lieutenant Thomas Boyd. The patrol had been out on a scout, and when he got back to the main army, Murphy told the commanders that the enemy had captured Boyd, according to Lieutenant Colonel Adam Hubley of the 11th Pennsylvania Regiment. In his journal entry for Sept. 13, Hubley wrote: "This Murphy is a noted marksman, and a great soldier, he having killed and scalped that morning . . . an Indian, which makes the three and 30th man of the enemy he has killed, as is well known to his officers (in) this war."

CHAPTER THREE

1776

'I am afraid', Loyalist Lawyer Confides to his Journal

In July 1776, many Pennsylvanians welcomed news of the Declaration of Independence, but many others did not, among them a 34-year-old lawyer named James Allen, who had grown up in Philadelphia. As 1776 progressed, Allen and his wife Elizabeth and their three small children left Philadelphia and moved 60 miles north of the city to their rural retreat—a two-story fieldstone house that he had built in 1770 on a hillside in present-day Allentown, then called Northampton Town.

Allen gave the Georgian-style residence, which had large lawns and gardens, a name: Trout Hall because members of his family had often fished for trout in nearby streams while vacationing there.

Historic marker in Allentown, Pennsylvania

Well-known, well-connected and well to do, Allen

James Allen lived in Trout Hall, Allentown, in 1777-78

belonged to an old, influential and conservative Pennsylvania family. His father William had once been mayor of Philadelphia, and William then had served as chief justice of the colony's Supreme Court for nearly a quarter of a century. James Allen's uncle, James Hamilton, had been governor of Pennsylvania, and his brother-in-law—the husband of his sister Anne—was John Penn, a grandson of William Penn. John Penn had served as the colony's governor through 1776.

Allen's story illustrates the struggle that many colonists had as events nudged the Continental Congress ever closer to breaking with Great Britain. The historic vote taken in the Pennsylvania State House on July 2, 1776, loudly declared American independency, but it also split the populace into three distinct groups: the Whigs, or Patriots, who welcomed independency; the

Loyalists, or Tories, who did no such thing; and the many who for a variety of reasons sought to remain neutral. The conflict split families, friends, neighbors, and communities.

Indeed, Allen's situation was far from unique. The course of political events in Pennsylvania, Massachusetts and London during the mid-1770s had strongly colored Allen's political beliefs and personal experiences. Initially, as he wrote in his journal on July 25, 1775, the lawyer appeared to encourage—and even endorse—the colonial revolt against the tyrannical policies and practices imposed by King George III and the British Parliament.

Musing privately, he said, ". . . God knows what will be the event of this war, as there seems to be a thorough determination on both sides to prosecute it." In Philadelphia, thoughtful people resolve to "keep up our spirits and, gloomy as things appear, prefer our situation to a mean acquiescence. It is a great and glorious cause. The eyes of Europe are upon us; if we fall, Liberty no longer continues an inhabitant of this globe: for England is running fast to slavery. The king is as despotic as any prince in Europe."

In 1775, as the Revolutionary War began, Allen's brother William served as lieutenant-colonel in a Pennsylvania regiment; and brother Andrew was a Pennsylvania delegate to the Continental Congress. By October 1775, James himself had joined a Philadelphia militia company commanded by a Captain John Shee. In early October, "I appeared in battalion in my uniform, as a private," Allen reported in his journal, expressing doubt "that this association will be very useful in defending the city . . . My inducement principally to join them is that a man is suspected who does not, and I choose to have a musket on my shoulders to be on a par with them; and I believe discreet people mixing with them may keep them in order."

In early 1776, the war moved closer to Pennsylvania. General William Howe abandoned Boston in March and sailed south to New York, with the American army trailing the British into the Middle Atlantic colonies.

In September 1776, prompted by "mere curiosity to view the state of both armies," Allen left Philadelphia and rode across New Jersey to Amboy, known today as Perth Amboy and situated on Raritan Bay just west of Staten Island. The British had troops on Staten Island, but the Continental Army and New Jersey militia controlled the New Jersey countryside.

"At Amboy," Allen wrote, "I visited my old friend General (Philemon) Dickinson and Major General (Hugh) Mercer, who commanded there . . ." Dickinson was a top-ranking officer the New Jersey Militia, and Mercer served in the Continental Army.

The lawyer traveled a short distance to the north, likely to Bergen Neck, a New Jersey peninsula immediately west of Upper New York Bay and Manhattan. "I . . . lodged with General (Daniel) Roberdeau and had a view of the city and harbor of New York. The sight was grand from the number of (British) ships in the harbor and shocking from the burnt ruins of that noble city; set on fire, as is supposed, by some of our army on their leaving it; at least as the enemy allege."

In this instance, it appears that Allen's use of the word *enemy* refers to the British.

Allen continued riding north along the New Jersey side of the Hudson River to Fort Lee "commanded by my old acquaintance General (James) Ewing, with whom I dined." Ewing was an officer in the Pennsylvania Militia.

Later that day Allen crossed the Hudson River, then frequently called the North River, and visited Washington's headquarters in New York. "General Washington received me with the utmost politeness; I lodged with him," Allen wrote.

"Next day," Allen said, "I recrossed the North River to Fort Lee and came through Hackensack . . . and thence through Morristown."

Allen returned to Pennsylvania, and "during October and November I remained at Trout Hall, a calm spectator of the civil war, but occasionally gave great offence to the violent Whigs in Northampton by entertaining the regular officers, our prisoners, and was often threatened on that account." The British prisoners that Allen entertained included a Richard Symes, a captain of the 52nd Regiment of Foot.

The actions of Allen's brothers in mid-December 1776 provided the Whigs with additional reasons to question Allen's loyalties. Andrew Allen had been a delegate to Congress, but stopped attending as Congress moved toward voting for independence. When Congress adopted the Declaration of Independence, William—whom James called Billy—resigned his commission in the Pennsylvania military. It is not clear when James Allen's own loyalties began shifting.

In late 1776, as the British and Hessians chased the Continental Army west across New Jersey, across the Delaware River and into eastern Pennsylvania, three of Allen's brothers—William, Andrew, and John—made their way to New Jersey, and sought sanctuary with the British. (Eventually, William organized, and commanded, a force of Pennsylvania Loyalists.) As James reported in his journal, few anticipated that the Continental soldiers would stop the British and the Hessians at the Delaware River. Many people assumed that General Howe would presently occupy Philadelphia.

As Allen reported, "When General Howe was expected in Philadelphia, a persecution of Tories . . . began; houses were broken open, (and) people imprisoned without any color of authority by private persons." A rumor spread throughout the city that "a list of 200 disaffected persons (was) made out, who were to be seized, imprisoned and sent off to North Carolina." It was said that the list included "our whole family."

The Allen family owned an iron works—the Union Forge—in Hunterdon County, New Jersey, near High Bridge, about 20 miles east of Easton, Pennsylvania. Fearful of being banished from Pennsylvania, Allen's brothers fled from Philadelphia, crossed into New Jersey and went to the family forge. Allen himself joined them there. "Soon after, against my judgment, they all went to Trenton and claimed protection from General Howe's army. From whence they went to New York where they now are, unhappily separated from their families and like to be so for some time."

For his part, James Allen returned to Philadelphia, but only long enough to take his family to Trout Hall, this time permanently. As he prepared to leave Philadelphia, Allen arranged for several Virginia delegates to the Continental Congress to lease in his residence there, along with "a great part of my furniture," for £150 a year. The delegates, incidentally, included Carter Braxton, who had signed the Declaration of Independence.

Although the Whigs, or patriots, around Northampton had organized a militia, Allen felt relieved to leave Philadelphia, "which from the current of politics, began to grow disagreeable. I thought myself happy in having so good a retreat in Northampton County."

Allen's relief was short lived: his day began with a start on Thursday, December 19.

"At 7 o'clock a.m., my house was surrounded by a guard of soldiers with fixed bayonets," Allen wrote later. "I got up, and when I came downstairs the officer who was at the front door produced a warrant from the Council of Safety to seize me and bring me before them."

The soldiers promptly took him back to Philadelphia.

Appearing before the committee, Allen found himself being examined by committee member Owen Biddle, who "said that they had received accounts of the unwillingness of the militia of Northampton County to march, that they knew my influence and property there, and were afraid of my being the cause of it, and added that my brothers being gone over to the enemy, the public would expect that I should be put on my parole and hoped I would have no objection to stay within six miles of Philadelphia."

Ever the lawyer, Allen gave a spirited defense: "I drew a picture of the state of the province, the military persecutions, the invasions of private property, imprisonments and abuses, that fell to the share of those whose consciences would not let them join in the present measures."

He pointed out that "two of their own ordinances authorizing field officers to invade and pillage our houses and imprison our persons on mere suspicion and concluded by saying that I was almost frightened into a determination of seeking the same protection that my brothers had done."

"Mr. Biddle," Allen said, "acknowledged the truth of what I said and excused the necessity of the present arbitrary measures by the divided state of America. I told him conciliatory measures would make more converts; that it was hard to forget we were once freemen who had lived under the happiest and freest government on earth; and I believed these violences inclined a majority of the people to wish for General Howe's arrival."

In the end, the Whigs permitted Allen to return to Trout Hall.

"At least, Mr. Allen may choose his place of residence," said committee member Timothy Matlack. To facilitate this, the Committee issued a document that allowed the lawyer to return to Northampton Town. Allen described it as "a certificate . . . wherein they set forth, my brothers' departure and the backwardness of our militia as reasons for sending for me, that I had given them satisfaction respecting my prudent conduct, that my conduct did not appear unfriendly to the cause of Liberty, nor inconsistent with the character of a gentleman; and I in return pledged my honor verbally not to say or do any thing injurious to the present cause of America."

With the committee's certificate in hand, "I spent five or six days in Philadelphia and near it with great pleasure at being in company with my relations and friends after so long (an) absence."

He found the city had changed significantly. "Philadelphia seemed almost deserted and resembled a Sunday in service time. The Quakers are almost the only people determined to remain there."

The city was also preparing to defend itself against attacks by the British. "They pressed all persons walking the streets to work in trenches surrounding the town; I was stopped and with difficulty got off by walking on and taking no notice of them," Allen said.

Allen returned to Trout Hall on December 28, a Saturday. He found life there "quiet and happy for some time," but the peaceable nature of country life was soon shattered.

One day, Allen's wife, Elizabeth, decided to visit a friend, Mrs. Bond. She took a daughter, Peggy, and one of Peggy's friends, Lyddy Duberry, in one of the family's three carriages, a light four-wheeled vehicle called a chariot that was driven by a man whom Allen identified only as Samson. As the carriage left Trout Hall and entered the street, it encountered a company of militia. "Samson endeavored to drive out of the road, but was stopped . . .," Allen wrote later. "The soldiers beat him with their muskets, and pushed at him with their bayonets, on which to defend himself he made use of his whip."

The children began screaming, and Elizabeth Allen begged "to be let out," but the militiamen, enraged by Samson's resistance, "pushed their bayonets into the chariot, broke the glass and pierced the chariot in three places," Allen said. "They also endeavored to overset it, while they (Mrs. Allen and the children) were within it."

As luck would have it, a man named David Deshler happened to be present. Deshler, commissioner of army supplies for Northampton County, "prevented it and led the horses on, by which means they escaped," Allen said. "Their design was to destroy the chariot."

Although the carriage sustained moderate damages, Elizabeth Allen, the girls and the driver weren't hurt. Allen himself didn't learn of the incident "till it was over and the company had marched on." Not long after, two militia officers—Major Boehm and Captain Buckhalter—came to Trout Hall. The major, whom Allen described as "a violent man," said he approved of the attack, and this sparked an angry exchange "between him and me, in which he attempted to draw his sword on me."

Writing on January 25, 1777, Allen said that the incident "has disturbed my peace, as I for some time expected the violence of the people, inflamed by some zealots would lead them to insult my person or attack my house. But as nothing of that kind has happened, I grow easy and hope it has blown over."

James Allen wrote in his journal only intermittently. His next entry was dated February 17, 1777. One passage is especially noteworthy:

"My particular situation has been of late very uneasy, owing to the battalion of militia of this district, assembling in the Town of Northampton, to the number of 600 men, where they continued a fortnight and marched off the day before yesterday. . . . They are generally disorderly, being under no discipline . . . Eight or nine parties of 15 or 20 men each came (to Tout Hall) to demand blankets, one party of which was very uncivil. But by prudence I escaped without any insult, having parted with 10 blankets. The principal officers behaved with great civility and . . . Col. Boehm . . . came to my house, to assure me he was innocent of the attack on my chariot and we buried the affair in oblivion. He assured me that the soldiers were ripe for doing some violence to my house, which he with difficulty prevented . . . Upon the whole I had great good fortune to escape without some injury from a riotous incensed soldiery, and am at present pretty easy on that head. Notwithstanding this, I am uneasy and wish to be in Philadelphia."

Allen's comments make it clear that in a mere two months, life at Trout Hall had become harsh. "My wife is often alarmed," he said. "I am afraid to converse with persons here, or write to my friends in Philadelphia, and a small matter, such as a letter intercepted or unguarded word, would plunge me into troubles."

He added: "I never knew how painful it is to be secluded from the free conversation of one's friends, the loss of which cannot be made up by any other expedients. I am considering whether I shall not leave this place in May and adjourn to Philadelphia . . . I should prefer continuing here, were I not in so conspicuous a point of light. It is odd to reflect that I am taking as much pains to be in obscurity, as others are to blaze in the public eye and become of importance."

CHAPTER FOUR

1777

The 'Hair Buyer' Rewards Indians Bringing Him Scalps

After his four-year indenture to a York farmer ended in 1773, a teenager named John Leeth went to the Ohio country. There he became the adopted son and brother of Delaware Indians in 1774, got caught up in the Revolutionary War, and in 1777 became acquainted with Lieutenant Colonel Henry Hamilton, the notorious British commandant at Fort Detroit known along the American frontier as The Hair Buyer.

Born in South Carolina in 1755 and orphaned at age five, John Leeth was the child of a Scottish father and a Virginia mother. As a boy, he spent two years as an apprentice to a tailor, who took him to Charleston, but after two years, Leeth ran away "from my master and his service."

In time, Leeth arrived in Pennsylvania, where he became the bound boy of a York farmer. He was 18 by the time his four-year indenture expired in 1773, and he struck out, presumably on foot, for Fort Pitt at Pittsburgh, some 230 mountainous miles to the west along the military road cut by the British in 1758.

"When my time of service was out, and I was free from my master, I bent my course to Fort Pitt . . . and hired myself to an Indian trader," Leeth said in his memoirs, an as-told-to account written by Ewel Jeffries and published in 1831.

Leeth's new employer took him deep into Ohio and assigned him to work at a trading post located in an Indian town along the Hocking River at present-day Lancaster, about 30 miles southeast of Columbus. The Hocking—known as the Hockhocking during the 1700s—flows into the Ohio River at the hamlet of Hockingport, about 70 miles southeast of Lancaster.

The trader and Leeth had arrived on the Hockhocking just in time for the start of Lord Dunmore's War, a frontier conflict touched off in 1774 when Governor Dunmore of Virginia sent an army to attack the Shawnees and Mingoes living in the Ohio River Valley.

As Leeth told his biographer: On April 10, "I was lying on some skins in my employer's store. An Indian boy came to me, and told me his father wanted to see me. I went with him; and when I came to the old man, he showed me a place to sit down. I took my seat with much wonder and surprise. As I could not yet understand Indian language, the old Indian, having a white woman for his wife, made her interpreter for us. He began with asking me if I had heard the news that a war had broken out between the whites and Indians; that the Shawnees had killed seven white men, and taken four prisoners; that the Virginians had taken Mingo Town, at Cross Creek, on the Ohio River. I answered him, that I had heard nothing of it."

Cross Creek enters the Ohio River at Steubenville, Ohio.

The youth didn't realize that the old Delaware intended to adopt him and planned to do so immediately.

"I answered . . . that I had heard nothing of it," Leeth said. "He asked me what I thought of the matter. With a trembling heart I informed him, I knew not what to think of it; that I had never done them any harm; I had no hand in the matter, and hoped they would take care of me. He then told me to rise and stand up on my feet. With the fearful expectation he intended to kill me immediately, I arose, and stood before him."

The old man pointed to his wife's breast and said, "Your mother has risen from the dead to give you suck." Then he laid his hand on his own breast and said, "Your father has also risen to take care of you, and you need not be afraid, for I will be a father to you."

The man "then embraced my neck, and called the chiefs around him; when they proceeded to divide the store-goods, spirits, and all that I had care of, among themselves."

In the fall, Lord Dunmore's soldiers fought a battle with the Shawnee Indians at the confluence of the Ohio and the Big Kanawha River, near present-day Point Pleasant, West Virginia, 40 miles down the Ohio River from Hockhocking.

"The Indians retreated with the loss of about twenty-five," Leeth said. "The army pursued and overtook them while they were crossing the river, and killed about twenty-five more; after which, the Indians returned to their habitations, and gave up the contest for that time.

"Some time after, news came that Dunmore was marching up the Hockhocking River, with an army; when some of the Indians proposed to kill me, and put me out of the way; but my late father—for he was a father to me, indeed—interfered, and prevented their horrid intention.

"They then commenced their flight from the towns, and took me with them, with my hands bound behind my back; they took me (on) a long and wearisome journey to their camp. Before we arrived at the camp, I formed a firm and settled resolution to make my escape, if any opportunity should offer, at which I made several attempts." But Leeth said he "was so closely watched" that escape wasn't possible.

When the Indians saw Lord Dunmore's soldiers return to Virginia, "my father gave me and his two sons our freedom, with a rifle, two pounds of powder, four pounds of lead; a blanket, shirt, match-coat, pair of leggings, etc. to each, as our freedom suits; and told us to shift for ourselves."

Leeth resumed the life of a fur trader, devoting his time to hunting, trapping and buying furs from native trappers. Within a few years, he found himself again caught up in war, this time the American Revolution. At one point, "I went with some of the Indian traders to Detroit; and when we arrived there, the British had the command and control of the place, furnishing the Indians with firearms, ammunition, the tomahawk and scalping-knife."

Fort Detroit

Located 20 miles up the Detroit River from Lake Erie, Fort Detroit was a British post in 1777. Its commandant, Lieutenant Colonel Henry Hamilton, was also the lieutenant governor of Canada.

Leeth made a second visit to Detroit, this time while employed by an established trader whose travels occasionally took him both to Sandusky, an Ohio settlement on the southern shore of Lake Erie, and to Detroit. Leeth helped the trader with some business at Detroit, but when the trader was ready to return to Sandusky, he directed Leeth to remain in Detroit in order to ship his trade goods "by water across the lake" to Sandusky since it was only 60 miles away from Detroit by water, but about 110 miles by land.

As Leeth said later: "Fort Detroit was then under martial law, and no person was permitted to go in or out without a pass from the governor . . . When I had made my arrangements to start with the goods, I went to the governor for a pass, informing him my employer had left orders with me to follow on after him . . . He asked where I wanted to take them. I told him to Sandusky. He then asked me what my employer gave me per month. I told him.

"He said it was not enough, and if I would join the Indian Department under his command, he would give me two dollars per day, and one and a half rations exclusively."

Hamilton was impressed that Leeth had lived with both the Shawnees and the Delawares and understood their languages. "He wanted me to interpret for them, and sometimes go to war with them against their enemies," Leeth said.

When Leeth declined on the grounds that he was "a very unhealthy, weakly youth," Hamilton remarked, "If you are not fit for the service, you are not fit for Sandusky; and you will stay where you are."

Unable to secure a pass from Hamilton, Leeth subsequently spent several months at Detroit.

During this time, the governor sent war parties of Indians allied with the British to raid American settlements in Kentucky, Virginia, West Virginia and Western Pennsylvania. During Leeth's stay in Detroit, the war parties returned with both white prisoners and scalps.

One day, Leeth watched as some soldiers moved several cannons out of the fort and arranged them on the bank of the Detroit River. A friend—"a young silver-smith"—came along "and asked me to walk with him, and see them fire the cannon." The two men walked over to where the soldiers had positioned the cannons.

"When we arrived there, we found Governor Hamilton, and several other British officers, who were standing and sitting around. Immediately after our arrival at the place, the Indians produced a large quantity of scalps; the cannon fired, the Indians raised a shout, and the soldiers waved their hats, with huzzas and tremendous shrieks, which lasted some time."

As the ceremony ended, the Indians presented the prisoners they had taken while raiding the American frontiers. Leeth counted "eighteen women and children . . . dreadfully mangled and emaciated; with their clothes tattered and torn to pieces in such a manner as not to hide their nakedness; their legs bare and streaming with blood; the effects of being torn with thorns, briars and brush."

At one point, Leeth looked over toward Colonel Hamilton. "The governor," he said, ". . . seemed to take great delight in the exhibition."

As did the Americans, the British paid a bounty on scalps brought in by their Indian allies. Warriors took scalps by cutting a section of skin, with hair attached, from the top of an enemy's head.

Leeth remained at Fort Detroit for several months. Eventually he obtained the pass he needed and he left. He told his biographer that he didn't know what had happened to the prisoners he had seen that day.

Henry Hamilton did such a thriving business in scalps that his nickname—The Hair Buyer—survives. In 1779 Virginia soldiers led by Colonel George Rogers captured him during an attack on a British fort along the Wabash River at present-day Vincennes, Indiana. The Virginians took him to Williamsburg, Virginia, where he was incarcerated for several months. Hamilton went to England, following a prisoner exchange, in 1781. He later returned to North America as the lieutenant governor and then deputy governor of Quebec from 1782 to 1785. He died of natural causes at age 62 in the West Indies.

CHAPTER FIVE

1777

Congress Flees as British Approach Philadelphia

All but banished from Philadelphia, Loyalist James Allen spent much of the second half of 1777 at Trout Hall in Northampton Town (present-day Allentown) and used his journal to carefully keep track of the war, which was rapidly becoming difficult for the Continental Army.

Writing on September 5, Allen reported, "General Howe with the grand army and fleet . . . is at length arrived in Chesapeake Bay and landed at the Head of Elk (near present-day Elkton, Maryland) . . . General Washington with a considerable strength of men including militia marched down and is now within a few miles of him; so that a battle is daily expected."

As Allen had projected, the fighting (today known as the Battle of Brandywine Creek) occurred six days later: Thursday, September 11, was "a day which will be long remembered, as both armies lay on Brandywine Creek," Allen said. ". . . General Howe began a general attack in front, which was made with great bravery by the grenadiers in the face of the artillery, and well defended. During this, Lord Cornwallis with 5,000 men crossed the creek five miles above and came on the flank of that part of the army commanded by General Sullivan who immediately threw down their arms and blankets and run [sic]. Soon after, the retreat became general. Nor did General Washington stop till he reached Chester where next day his army collected."

General William Howe

The distance between Chadds Ford and Philadelphia is only 30 miles, but it took the British 14 days to travel that far. By September 23, the army was still 11 miles west of the city, and rumors spread that rebels would burn the town rather than let it fall into enemy hands. "In the evening, the inhabitants were exceedingly alarmed by an apprehension of the city being set on fire," Robert Morton, a Philadelphia teenager from a Loyalist family, wrote in his diary.

The youth kept a running tally of events that happened as the British closed in. On September 24, for example, "a number of horses were taken out of the city to prevent them from falling into the hands of the enemy." That night Morton joined other Philadelphians who long after midnight were out "patrolling the streets for fear of fire. Two men were taken up who acknowledged their intentions of doing it."

When the British and Hessians reached the Schuylkill River, the Continentals didn't challenge them. As Allen said, "General Washington suffered General Howe to cross the Swedes Ford, without any opposition, and he entered Philadelphia on Thursday, the 25th of September."

The account penned by Morton, who witnessed the event, provided more details: "About 11 o'clock a.m. Lord Cornwallis with his division of the British and Auxiliary Troops amounting to about 3,000, marched into this city . . . to the great relief of the inhabitants who have too long suffered the yoke of arbitrary power."

The teenager also identified several Philadelphia Loyalists who accompanied Cornwallis. In faraway Trout Hall, Allen had no way of knowing, but the Loyalists included two of his brothers, Andrew and William.

As the Tories welcomed Howe, the Whigs, or Patriots, fled. With the British west of the city, many hurried north, taking a somewhat roundabout route that literally took them past Trout Hall. Heading north and following well-worn dirt roads wide enough for wagons, they first went to Bethlehem, a religious commune operated by the Moravian Brethren that was 55 miles from Philadelphia.

Founded in 1741, Bethlehem occupied a hilltop overlooking the Lehigh River. The Moravians had erected a variety of large stone buildings in the heart of their settlement. As members of

The Moravians built a blacksmith shop on this site in Bethlehem, Pennsylvania, in 1750. It was part of the main settlement when Congress came to town in 1777. Photo shows a 2004 reconstruction of the smithy based on archaeological and Moravian records.

Congress and officers of the Continental Army arrived, they quickly thought up uses for the dormitory-style structures.

The Moravians had learned on September 16 that General Washington had ordered the army to move its supplies to Bethlehem. Pacifists, the Moravians had objected immediately "that Bethlehem was no fit place for storing supplies, . . . but all in vain," the anonymous diarist wrote. That day, 36 wagons hauling military goods crossed the Lehigh River and lumbered into town. "The wagons were unloaded near the tile-kilns (along Monocacy Creek), and a guard of 40 men posted."

Over the next ten days, some 900 military wagons rolled into town. Many were parked behind the Sun Tavern, which was near the community's

Dr. William Shippen Jr.

principal buildings. "With them came a crowd of low women and thieves, so that we had to maintain a watch at the tavern," the scribe wrote.

On September 19, a Friday, the leaders of Bethlehem received a letter from Dr. William Shippen Jr., one of the Continental Army's chief medical officers. The Congress, Shippen wrote, had ordered him "to send my sick and wounded soldiers to your peaceable village. . . . Your large buildings must be appropriated to their use. We will want room for 2,000 at Bethlehem, Easton, Northampton, etcetera. And you may expect them on Saturday or Sunday."

On Saturday, September 20, the Brethren's House—a four-story structure built in 1748 that served as the residence of unmarried men—was vacated. It quickly became a military hospital. On Sunday, September 21, "towards evening the sick and wounded from Bristol began to arrive, and the influx of strangers became greater, so that the Sun Tavern could not hold them." On September 22, "more sick and wounded arrived, which filled up the house," according to records kept by the Moravian Church.

The American casualties included a young officer wounded in the battle on the Brandywine—the 20-year-old Marquis de La Fayette, who held the rank of major general. The Frenchman had

Lafayette wounded at the Battle of Brandywine

been shot through the leg by British soldiers during a charge. At first, the Marquis was lodged in the tavern, but the two Moravian women assigned to be his nurses—Mrs. Barbara Boeckel and her daughter Liesel—soon arranged for him to be moved to their private residence near the tavern.

As the days went by, John Hancock, Samuel Adams, and 14 other Congressional delegates arrived in Bethlehem. Some of the army surgeons, seeing a pressing need for "an additional building for the sick, . . . suggested the Sisters' or Widows' Houses," but an influential Moravian clergyman, the Rev. John Ettwein, convinced them to drop the idea.

"In the evening arrived 50 troopers and 50 infantry, with the archives and other papers of Congress, from Trenton via Easton," the Bethlehem diarist wrote.

The Moravian settlement had made a favorable impression on some of the congressmen, who asked if "we would consent to their making Bethlehem their headquarters during the war." The suggestion didn't sit well, and "It was by much persuasion . . . that we induced them to abandon that idea."

On September 24, "the whole of the heavy baggage of the army, in a continuous train of 700 wagons, direct from camp, arrived under escort of 200 men, commanded by Col. (William) Polk, of North Carolina. They encamped on the south side of the Lehigh, and in one night destroyed all our buckwheat and the fences around the fields." The diarist added, "The wagons, after unloading, return to Trenton for more stores."

Before leaving Philadelphia, the rebels had removed many objects that the British could have used. "Among the things brought here were the church bells from Philadelphia." The bells included what later became known as the Liberty Bell. (The State House, whose belfry it adorned, later became known as Independence Hall.) With little fanfare, the bell reached Bethlehem in a horse-drawn wagon, "and the wagon in which was loaded the State House bell, broke down in the street, and had to be unloaded."

Eventually, the bell was taken to Northampton Town (Allentown) and hidden in a church about half a mile from James Allen's residence, Trout Hall. Allen didn't mention the bell in his journal entry for October 1. He did, however, note that "many of the Congress passed by this place

(Northampton) and are since assembled, together with the officers of this government, at Lancaster."

Elaborating, Allen added: "Since the battle of Brandywine, many thousand wagons (have) passed my door and are continually passing in great numbers. All the baggage of our army is at Bethlehem and here; and what with hospitals and artificers, these little towns are filled. Every day some of the inhabitants of Philadelphia are coming up to settle here. The road from Easton to Reading, by my house, is now the most travelled in America. The Congress have removed to York over Susquehanna and our (Pennsylvania) Council and Assembly sit at Lancaster."

Even as Howe and Cornwallis took over Philadelphia, the British began planning a military effort to break Continental control of the lower Delaware River. Just below Philadelphia on the Pennsylvania shore, Fort Mifflin stood. Across the Delaware, on the New Jersey shore, facing it, was Fort Mercer. Washington regarded the two forts, which were constructed in 1776, as essential assets in blocking the Delaware to British ships.

In ordering Lieutenant Colonel Samuel Smith to take a detachment of 200 Continental soldiers into New Jersey to reinforce Fort Mercer in late September, Washington stated, "The keeping of the fort is of very great importance, and I rely strongly on your prudence, spirit and bravery for a vigorous and persevering defense."

The Americans had placed obstructions in the Delaware in the vicinity of this fort. Made of sunken logs with pointed ends, they were called

"Chevaux de frize." Their purpose was to impale the hull of British warships coming up the river.

Several weeks later, Washington referred to these defensive assets in describing Fort Mercer as "an important post (that) commands and defends the Chevaux de frize." He added: "Unless kept in our possession, our vessels of war must quit their station and thereby leave the enemy at liberty to weigh the Chevaux de frize and open the free navigation of the river."

In early October, Washington learned from the contents of "two intercepted letters" that General William Howe had sent a significant force to dislodge the rebels from these forts. In effect, the British commander had divided his army, and Washington saw this as "a favorable opportunity . . . to make an attack upon the troops, which were at and near German Town."

Germantown was a village about 10 miles northwest of Philadelphia, and Washington and his officers decided that the Continental Army and the militia units accompanying it would move close to the British camp during the night of October 3-4, in order to attack early on the morning of October 4. "The militia of Maryland and Jersey under Generals (William) Smallwood and (David) Forman were to march by the Old York Road and fall upon the rear of their right," Washington said.

He continued: "We marched about 7 o'clock the preceding evening (October 3) and General Sullivan's advanced party . . . attacked their picket at Mount Airy . . . about sunrise the next morning, which presently gave way, and his (Sullivan's) main body . . . soon engaged the light infantry and

Battle of Germantown

other troops, encamped near the picket, which they forced from the ground, leaving their baggage."

According to a draft of Washington's October 5 letter to Congress, the battle took place in "a thick, heavy fog which prevented our seeing more than fifty yards."

"The Jersey Militia . . . under General (David) Forman and the Maryland Militia with some (en)listed troops under General Smallwood were on the left wing of the whole army," reported Colonel Asher Holmes of the Monmouth Militia. "We drove the enemy when we first made the attack, but by the thickness of the fog the enemy got into our rear."

The men in Captain Phillips' Company of the Hunterdon County Militia found themselves in the thick of the fighting. Two of the men from Coryell's Ferry on the Delaware—Charlie Pidcock and Amos Peters—were positioned near each other. As all soldiers did, they used ramrods to load their muskets. Years later, Peters said that he clearly remembered "Pidcock breaking his ramrod in ramming down a cartridge and was forced to borrow one to get it down."

Private Joseph Plumb Martin of the 8th Connecticut Regiment tells what happened elsewhere on the battlefield. "Our brigade moved off to the right into the fields," Martin said. "We saw a body of the enemy drawn up behind a rail fence on our right flank. We immediately formed in line and advanced upon them. Our orders were not to fire till we could see the buttons upon their clothes."

The rebels advanced rapidly, routing their foes. "The enemy were driven quite through their camp. They left their kettles in which they were cooking their breakfasts on the fires, and some of their garments were lying on the ground, which the owners had not time to put on," Martin said.

For some time, the Americans held the upper hand. Then things turned. "The enemy were retreating before us until the first division that was engaged had expended their ammunition. Some of the men unadvisedly calling out that their ammunition was spent, the enemy were so near that they overheard them," the soldier said.

On the Pennsylvania Line, at 5 o'clock "the attack began from right to left," reported Lieutenant James McMichael. "We drove the enemy for near three miles with the utmost precipitation, but the Maryland militia under the command of General Smallwood, not coming to flank us in proper time, together with the cowardice of the 13th Virginia regiment, gave the enemy an opportunity of coming round our left flank."

In a letter written to his sister Sarah on October 6, Colonel Asher said, "Our line of battle was broke, and we were obliged to retreat."

Asher added, "The attack was made by different divisions in different quarters, nearly at the same time, but the morning being very foggy was much against us, and the severe firing added to the thickness of the air, which prevented our seeing far, therefore a great disadvantage to us."

The Continental regulars and the militiamen withdrew as quickly as they could, and a day's retreat took them about 30 miles northwest of Philadelphia, where they camped along the Perkiomen Creek. It had not been a good day.

"It was disagreeable to have to leave the field, when we had almost made a conquest," Lieutenant McMichael said in an October 5 journal entry written in the camp at Perkiomen. He added: "I had marched in 24 hours 45 miles, and in that time fought four hours, during which we advanced so furiously through buckwheat fields that it was almost an unspeakable fatigue."

General Washington didn't regard the defeat as a serious one. As he said in an October 5 letter to Colonel Smith: "We surprised them and threw their whole army into confusion, and had not the fogginess of the morning prevented us from seeing the advantage we had gained, it would have ended in a complete victory, as they themselves have confessed."

CHAPTER SIX

1777

Pennsylvania Soldiers Have Dire Need of Shoes, Shirts

———•◆•———

As the Continental Army settled into winter quarters at Valley Forge in late December 1777, General George Washington informed the Congress that he "had no more than 8,200 (soldiers) in camp fit for duty." At the same time, "we have, by a field return this day made, no less than 2,898 men now in camp unfit for duty because they are barefoot and otherwise naked."

Washington described the situation aptly. Decades later, an elderly man named Joseph Plumb Martin remembered having endured similar conditions during his Valley Forge service in a Connecticut regiment. In the weeks before they gathered along the Schuylkill River northwest of Philadelphia, the men were "not only starved but naked," Martin wrote in his memoirs. "The greatest part were not only shirtless and barefoot, but destitute of all other clothing, especially blankets." The old soldier recalled that one day, "I procured a small piece of raw cowhide and made myself a pair of moccasins, which kept my feet (while they lasted) from the frozen ground."

It was against this backdrop that Brigadier General Anthony Wayne waged a frustrating effort throughout the winter of 1777-78 to obtain suitable clothing for the soldiers of the Pennsylvania Line.

General Anthony Wayne

As his soldiers shivered along the Schuylkill, Wayne wrote on February 10, 1778: "Hundreds of our poor worthy fellows have not a single rag of a shirt, but are obliged to wear their waistcoats next (to) their skins and to sleep in them at nights."

Months earlier—in November 1777—Wayne had proclaimed his conviction that well-dressed soldiers performed much better than did shabbily-dressed troops: "For my own part I would sooner risk my life . . . at the head of five thousand troops neatly uniformed than with double that number equally armed and disciplined, covered with rags and crawling with vermin."

At the time, the Congress had urged the states to provide suitable clothing for the troops that they had sent to join Washington's army. Well-to-do officers, of course, were free to purchase their own uniforms, but many officers as well as rank-and-file soldiers were too poor to do this.

To be certain, there were plenty of suitable clothes in Philadelphia less than 25 miles to

Encampment at Valley Forge

the south east. It was one of the wealthiest cities in North America. But the British army had marched into Philadelphia in two months before, in late September, thereby eliminating the city as a source of supplies for the Continentals.

At the same time, the American soldiers—regular troops as well as Pennsylvania militiamen—did all they could to prevent British foraging parties to obtain food and other supplies from the countryside surrounding Philadelphia. As historian Robert Proud, who lived in Philadelphia during the winter of 1777-78, said in a letter to a relative in early 1778: "This city (is) being still, as it were, besieged by the rebel militia supported by Washington's army, who, in small parties around it in the country, do everything in their power to prevent provisions coming in." Their tactics involve "plundering the Inhabitants of what they can find . . . and burning such part of the hay, corn, and forage around us as they cannot carry off." They do this "to prevent, as they say, it's coming into the hands of the English. These parties always run away when the king's troops go out after them, and return again when they retreat."

In camp at Valley Forge, Wayne had expected Pennsylvania state officials to furnish the clothing. When they failed to do so, the general didn't mince words. The lack of suitable clothing, he wrote on February 10, 1778, has "our men . . . falling sick in numbers every day, contracting vermin and dying in hospitals in a condition shocking to humanity." The general added sarcastically: "The clothier general informed me when I was at Lancaster that there were shirts in plenty at camp. I find he was mistaken . . . I have not been able to draw a single shirt from the store."

Wayne had been gravely concerned about the ragged condition of the Pennsylvania soldiers even before the army established winter camp at Valley Forge. On December 4, 1777, for example, Colonel John Bayard had quoted him at length in a letter written to Thomas Wharton, Jr., the president of the Supreme Executive Council of Pennsylvania. More than a third of the men in Wayne's command, Bayard wrote, "have neither breeches, shoes, stockings, blankets, and are by that means rendered unable to do duty, or indeed keeping the field. It is truly distressing to see these poor naked fellows encamped on bleak hills."

Bayard was an officer in a Pennsylvania regiment, the 2nd Philadelphia, as well as a member of the Pennsylvania General Assembly. He wrote his letter at Plymouth, a Quaker community about 15 miles northwest of Philadelphia.

"General Wayne assures us if he had not sent out officers to buy clothing of every kind through the country, his troops must have been naked," the colonel told Wharton, frequently referred to as the president of the State of Pennsylvania. Despite the seediness of their uniforms, "when any prospect of an action with the enemy (develops), these brave men appear full of spirits and eager for engaging."

On December 28, Wayne wrote directly to Wharton, again advising him that "at this inclement season one third of our troops are totally destitute of either shoes, stockings, shirts or blankets, so that unless they receive an immediate supply of these necessary articles, sickness, death and desertion will be the inevitable consequence."

Before long, even General Washington himself was writing to Wharton, reporting "how destitute the men in the field are in point of clothing." In a letter dated January 19 from Valley Forge, the commanding general explained: "I had sent out officers from every regiment to procure clothing for their men, and they were collecting considerable quantities when Col. Bayard and Mr. Young, a deputation from the (Pennsylvania) assembly, waited upon me, and desired me to call in the officers, informing me that they had appointed commissioners in every county to purchase necessaries for the army, which would be a mode more agreeable to the inhabitants, than if done in the military way."

Washington had seen the merit in what Bayard and Young said during their early December visit, but six weeks had passed without any results. The general remarked a bit impatiently: "What these commissioners have done I do not know, but no clothing has yet come to the army through their hands. General Wayne informed me that he understood it was collected and stored at Lancaster, and he went up about ten days ago to enquire into the matter."

Three weeks later, on February 10, Washington again wrote to Wharton, reporting that when General Wayne returned from Lancaster in January, he "brought a tolerable supply for the two brigades under his command; but the 3rd, 6th, 9th, 12th, and 13th regiments are in great distress, and are the more uneasy and discontented as they see their companions are provided for."

Washington suggested that if Pennsylvania authorities had secured additional apparel in the weeks since Wayne's trip to Lancaster, "what clothing is collected may be immediately sent down."

To Wharton's embarrassment, Washington also disclosed that a deputy quartermaster general in the Continental Army had discovered that Pennsylvania had a large stash of military clothes at Reading, about 40 miles northwest of Valley Forge.

The officer, Colonel J. H. Lutterloh, "informs me that he found a considerable quantity of clothing collected at Reading, waiting for an order to be sent forward." Washington wrote. "This being the particular property of your state, I did not think myself at liberty to interfere with it, but I hope you will immediately order it to camp." It appears that Wharton was unaware of this cache.

Since both Reading and Valley Forge were along the Schuylkill River, "It may come down by water and save the labor and expense of wagons," Washington said.

Nothing happened—again. As April arrived, General Wayne was still writing to Wharton, complaining yet again about his soldiers' pressing need for adequate clothing.

"For God's sake, endeavor to do something for us," Wayne exclaimed at one point. "The season is now arrived that requires every attention to keep the troops healthy, and nothing will be more conducive to it than clean linen."

General Wayne emphasized that "although tolerable with regard to shoes, stockings, and hats, we are but wretchedly provided in other respects, particularly as to shirts. . . . Near one third of my men . . . have no kind of shirt under Heaven, and scarcely a man in the division with more than one, nor have I been able to draw any during this whole winter."

A full four months into the controversy, many soldiers in Wayne's command still lacked even basic articles of clothing. Like a bulldog, the general wouldn't let go. Writing to Wharton once again, this time on April 16, Wayne enclosed a list of the soldiers in two brigades of Pennsylvania troops. "The sick now in camp . . . have been laid up for want of clothing, except in a few Instances. There is scarcely one of them that has a shirt."

Wayne reported that a "Mr. Donaldson, of York" believes that "he could supply us with three or four hundred per week, and that he has linen now on hand sufficient to make six hundred, and that he can procure a large quantity if properly empowered and supplied with cash."

The general asked Wharton to give Donaldson whatever funds he needed to get the clothes made. "We shall certainly want in the whole 9,000 shirts and 9,000 pair of overalls," Wayne said. By this time it was spring.

If Wayne managed finally to secure clothes for soldiers in his part of the Pennsylvania Line, troops in other sections remained without. On April 18, Wayne reported that "Colonel Butler of the 9th Pennsylvania Regiment, among other business, wants clothing for his regiment. I wish him to be indulged, if it can be done without prejudice to the other part of the line."

Wayne added that since November 1777, one supplier alone, Paul Zantzinger of York, had provided "about five hundred and fifty coats; two hundred waistcoats; three hundred and eighty pair of breeches, and an equal number of stockings, about one hundred pair of shoes, and several hundred hats."

These articles had been distributed among many regiments, "and has only in part clothed about one fourth of them," Wayne said.

Five regiments—the 3rd, 6th, 9th, 12th and 13th—had received the lion's share of these clothes "which, I believe, is rather more than came to the share of the other nine. I therefore wish that all such clothing as may be ready, was sent together, and I will undertake to see impartial justice done to the whole."

Wayne raised the issue of clothing yet again in a May 4 letter to Wharton. "I know it must be distressing to your Excellency to hear so many repetitions of our wants, but whatever pain it may give you, I hourly experience more from viewing the distress of worthy fellows who are conscious of meriting some attention. They unhappily think any change will be for the better, and too many have therefore risked desertion."

The reason that so many of the soldiers in Pennsylvania's regiments were listed as ill "is for want of clothing, being too naked to appear on the parade," Wayne said. "Our officers in particular are in a most wretched condition."

The historical record isn't clear, but it's doubtful that Wayne's soldiers were properly clad by the time the British Army evacuated Philadelphia in mid-June, and crossed New Jersey heading for New York City. Had the British stayed in Philadelphia during the following winter, no one knows what might have happened to the American Revolutionary army.

After the British withdrew from Philadelphia, the Continentals quickly left Valley Forge—on the attack. "We marched immediately in pursuit," Private Joseph Plumb Martin, the Connecticut volunteer, wrote in his memoirs. "We crossed the Delaware at Carroll's (Coryell's) Ferry above Trenton, and encamped a day or two between that town and Princeton."

The Americans caught up with and attacked the British at present-day Freehold, New Jersey, about twenty miles due south of Staten Island, New York. The fighting there, which involved a total of more than 20,000 troops, is today known as the Battle of Monmouth. Wayne and the Pennsylvanians fought spiritedly, but the battle ended

Tories, Terror, and Tea

George Washington at the Battle of Monmouth

in a draw. The British continued their withdrawal toward New York City.

In his memoirs, Martin referred to all the troops in the Continental Army when he said, "On our march from the Valley Forge, through the Jerseys, and at the . . . Battle of Monmouth, a fourth part of the troops had not a scrap of anything but their ragged shirt flaps to cover their nakedness, and were obliged to remain so long after."

As for Joseph Plumb Martin himself, "I had picked up a few articles of light clothing during the past winter, while among the Pennsylvanian farmers, or I should have been in the same predicament."

CHAPTER SEVEN

1777
'An Indian War Is Now Raging Around Us in its Utmost Fury'

When a frontier preacher, Philip Vickers Fithian, traveled along the Susquehanna River's West Branch during the summer of 1775, he found farmers as well as village residents engaged in peacetime pursuits. They were busily establishing and enlarging farms, organizing congregations and attracting new settlers. True, people eagerly awaited the post riders who brought news about the latest efforts of the newly organized Continental Army against the British army at Boston, but Massachusetts was hundreds of miles away, and Fithian's daily entries depicted the region as a tranquil, pastoral place far removed from the American Revolutionary War.

Stopping along the river at present-day Watsontown, Pennsylvania, then called Warriors Run, to preach on Sunday, July 16, Fithian found that construction of the meeting house hadn't been completed, so "I preached from a wagon, the only one which was present. The people sat on a rising ground before me. It looks odd to see the people sitting among the bushes. All were attentive. And there were many present."

On Wednesday, July 19, the preacher was in Northumberland when "two wagons, with goods, cattle, women, tools, etcetera, went through town today from East Jersey, on their way to Fishing Creek up this river, where they are to settle," he wrote.

To be sure, Fithian's daily journal also reflected the grimmer aspects of everyday life along the Susquehanna: the July 10 incident in which a farm woman "reaping in the harvest field was bit by a snake! She lies now in great distress, swelled up into her back and shoulders" and the July 23 funeral of a 3-year-old boy who suffocated after attempting to swallow some rye that his father had just harvested.

People eagerly awaited the post riders who brought news of the fighting at Boston, but in the main, Fithian's daily entries depicted the region as a pastoral place far removed from the horrors of war.

A bachelor, the 28-year-old itinerant preacher indulged in such peace-time frivolities as berry-picking in the company of eligible young women from the settlements. On July 27—a Saturday—in the vicinity of present-day Lock Haven, Fithian and another young man, identified only as "Mr. Gilaspee," took Miss Betsey Fleming and Miss Jenny Reed across the West Branch in a canoe "and went up a very high and steep mountain to gather huckleberries. . . . We found them in the greatest plenty, low bushes bended to the ground

"Fort Augusta in the Snow" by Michael P. Roush. (Courtesy Michael P. Roush)

with their own weight." On the return trip the canoe capsized in shallow water, spilling all the berries and dunking the foursome.

Blaming Gilaspee for the mishap, the girls splashed him until he was thoroughly soaked. "We then waded, dripping, to the shore," Fithian wrote.

Within three years, all this had changed. British officers at faraway Fort Niagara along Lake Ontario had begun sending war parties of Iroquois and Delaware Indians on raids against the frontier settlements. As a result, the Susquehanna Valley, along with much of Frontier Pennsylvania farther west, had become a darker, fearful place.

As early as September 10, 1777, Colonel Samuel Hunter, the commander at Fort Augusta, fretted about the possibility of an Indian war. For starters, he had a huge region to defend. Established in 1772, Northumberland County stretched across much of northern Pennsylvania.

Tories, Terror, and Tea

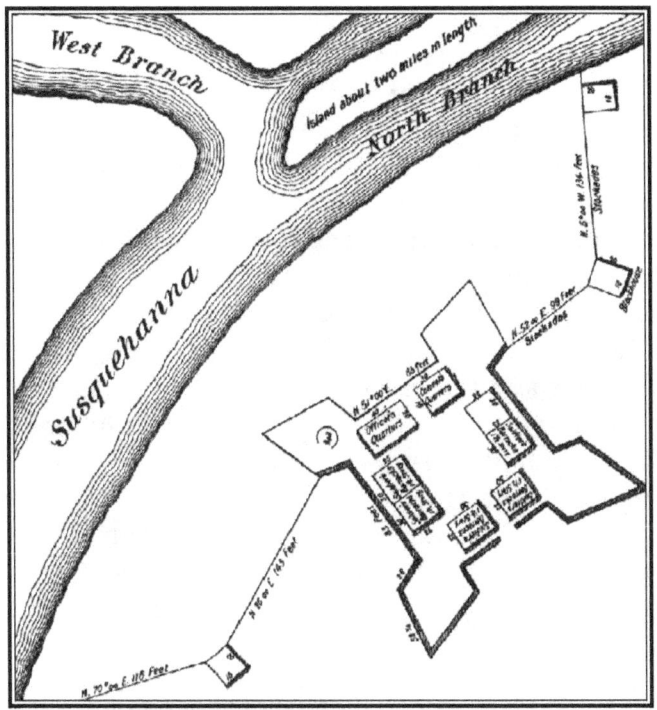

Fort Augusta, Sunbury, PA

Militia troops stood ready to defend against any attacks, but "we are badly off in this county for want of arms and ammunition," Hunter wrote to George Bryan, vice president of Pennsylvania's Executive Council in Philadelphia. He noted that he had already advised a member of the council "to endeavor to procure five hundred stand of arms, which will be very much wanted in case we are invaded here by ye savages."

Word had come down the West Branch to Sunbury that Indians had been "seen about forty miles above the Great Island, and a colonel of our militia, one Cookson Long, set off last Saturday with a party of men to know if they had any hostile intentions," Hunter told Bryan.

This location put the Indians at the spot where a strategic Indian trail—the Sinnemahoning—met the West Branch. This path followed the Sinnemahoning Creek and was frequently used by natives—peaceable ones as well as hostiles headed toward the Pennsylvania settlements from the Allegheny River Valley. A rumor circulating in the Great Island settlements held that there might be "a large party . . . of Indians," perhaps numbering two hundred. If true, that would suffice "to alarm that part of the country," Hunter said.

Six weeks later—on October 27—Hunter reported that "nothing has happened concerning the Indians or the frontiers of this county since the militia went there" in early September. Nevertheless, fearful of Indian attacks, "upwards of five hundred . . . men, women and children (had) assembled at three different places on the West Branch . . . at the mouth of Bald Eagle (Creek), Ante's Mill (across from present-day Jersey Shore) and Lycoming." Also, some friendly Indians had come to the settlements with their families "whom I allow provisions while they stay."

Meanwhile, "Colonel John Kelly . . . is out at this present time with a party of fifty men and an Indian called Job Chilloway to reconnoiter and make discoveries of any enemy Indians if within fifty miles of the Great Island. . . . If his (Kelly's) report is favorable, it will be a means of encouraging the poor settlers to go back to their respective habitations," Hunter said.

Earlier in the autumn, as the British army prepared to occupy Philadelphia, the U.S. and Pennsylvania governments headed toward the Susquehanna River, the national government to York and the state government to Lancaster. Hence, Hunter sent his October 27 letter to Thomas Wharton, president of the state's Executive Council, to Lancaster. He reported that he had received 750 pounds cash to pay members of the Northumberland County militia then on duty in the county's frontier. He also acknowledged receipt of 500 pounds of gunpowder and 1,200 pounds of lead—"but no rifle guns, which is one material article much wanted in this county."

Thomas Wharton (1735-1778), by Charles Willson Peale

If the time had come to prepare against attacks by pro-British Indians, the Whigs controlling the state government also had decided it was now necessary to disarm Loyalists living within the state. Hunter noted that he had previously been ordered "to disarm all persons in this county that refuses (*sic*) to take the oath of allegiance." He explained that "at that time I could not with any propriety take the arms from several on the frontier that was willing to stand in their own defense against the savages, yet never said they would not take the oath." These men had said that they "wanted time to consider . . . it until the

Iroquois war parties that raided the Pennsylvania frontier during the American Revolutionary War met in this Seneca Council house, now located at Letchworth State Park in western New York. It originally stood at Canadea on the Genesee River.

election, but as that time is passed and a number (is) not willing to take said oath, your orders will immediately be put in execution."

Writing from Bedford, 200 miles to the west, on Nov. 27, Thomas Smith and George Woods reported, "an Indian war is now raging around us in its utmost fury." War parties had struck along Stony Creek, Dunning's Creek and at various places in the mountains. "A small party went out into Morrison's Cove scouting, and—unfortunately—divided. The Indians discovered one division and out of eight killed seven and wounded the other." Near present-day Hollidaysburg, some 30 miles north of Bedford, hostiles "wounded one (settler) and killed some children by Frankstown. . . . Had they not providentially been discovered in the night, and a party went out and fired on them, they would in all probability have destroyed a great part of that settlement in a few hours."

Many homesteaders had already fled from the region. "We keep out ranging parties, in which we go out by turns, but all that we can do that way is but weak and ineffectual," Woods and Smith said. They suggested that "a small number of select men would be of more real service to guard the frontiers than six times that number of people unused to arms or the woods."

Equally disturbing were verbal reports that reached the Pennsylvania Council of Safety in Lancaster from even farther west. In Westmoreland County, "an extent of 60 miles has been evacuated to the savages, full of stock, corn, hogs and poultry," the council said in a November 14 letter to Congress. ". . . There is . . . reason to fear the ravages will extend to Bedford and along the frontier."

The council said it intended to order the Bedford County militia to march immediately to relieve the Westmoreland settlements. "We find they are greatly deficient in the articles of arms, and especially ammunition and flints. In Fort Ligonier, when our informants left it, there was not more than 40 pounds of powder and 15 pounds of lead. Flints are sold at a dollar apiece."

The actions ordered by the Council of Safety appear to have done little to stop or even slow the attacks.

"They have . . . continued to destroy and burn houses, barns and grain," Archibald Lochret wrote to President Wharton on December 6.

In an obvious reference to the east-west military road that British General John Forbes had built across western Pennsylvania during the French and Indian War, Lochret said that many settlers remained on their farms along the north side of "the Great Road." He reported that these people had a dire need that didn't involve either guns or ammunition: "They have no salt to lay up meat, of which there is a great plenty. Their grain is all burned and destroyed on the north of Conemaugh (River). If there is no store of provision for next summer, and the people (are) hindered from getting spring crops, the country is undoubtedly broke up."

Lochret said that a scouting party out of Westmoreland had skirmished successfully with a war party on its way back to Indian country after it had raided Western Pennsylvania settlements. The fighting occurred near Kittanning on the Alleghany River, and the militiamen "retook six horses the savages had taken from the suffering frontiers."

Lochret added: "I have sent five Indian scalps taken by one of our scouting party."

During an ordinary year, winter's approach often signaled a seasonal cessation of Indian attacks, but the winter of 1777-78 proved to be an exception. In Eastern Pennsylvania, native warriors persisted in raiding the Northumberland frontier into January. "There has been two men killed and scalped by them lately near the Great Island" in the Susquehanna River's West Branch, Colonel Hunter reported from Fort Augusta on January 14, adding: "One (raid on) the 23d of last month, near the mouth of Pine Creek, . . . occasioned the Inhabitants to assemble in two or three different places . . . for their own preservation."

In early January, hostiles "killed and scalped" a settler "about two miles above the Great Island." "Eleven Indians (were) seen, but our people pursued them (as there had fell a snow which enabled our men to track), and killed two of the Indians. The others fled, and was pursued a great ways, but our men could not come up with them, and they turned back to their families," the militia commander said.

CHAPTER EIGHT

1778

Shortage of Lead Triggers Severe Scarcity of Bullets

"Run, Janet! Run!"

Adam Holliday, a settler who lived along the Juniata River, shouted these words to his daughter as Indian warriors came across the field.

The American Revolutionary War was in progress, and Holliday, for whom present-day Hollidaysburg is named, knew that the Indians were siding with the British.

Janet and her three brothers—James, Pat and John—had been helping their father work on the family farm when the warriors suddenly emerged from the woods.

As Holliday hurriedly placed John and James on a horse, Janet and Pat started to run across the field. An Indian wielding a tomahawk raced after her.

That's when the father desperately shouted to Janet, but "the cruel savage repeated his words in derision, as he sunk the deadly tomahawk into her brain," wrote I. D. Rupp in his

1847 history of settlements along the Juniata and Susquehanna.

Although Holliday and his two younger boys escaped, the Indians also caught and killed his eldest son Pat.

About 16 miles north of Hollidaysburg, there was a small lead mine, tucked away in the Sinking Valley east of present-day Altoona. Demand for lead bullets increased during the Revolution, and by early 1778, there was a shortage throughout Pennsylvania.

Writing from York in February 1778, Major General John Armstrong reported "that the mine ought . . . be seized by" the state and worked to produce lead so badly needed for ammunition. "I'm of opinion that a few faithful laborers may be sufficient," Armstrong wrote.

A Philadelphia merchant named Daniel Roberdeau was a member of the Continental Congress, then meeting in York because the British army had occupied Philadelphia. Roberdeau, who also held the rank of brigadier general in the Pennsylvania military, left Congress and headed for present-day Blair County to take charge of the mine.

Along the way he stopped in Carlisle, where Lieutenant John Carothers, commandant of the Cumberland County militia, cautioned him that Indian attacks could well

Major General John Armstrong

jeopardize any progress at the mine. Carothers assigned a company of 40 militia soldiers to accompany Roberdeau.

The timing couldn't have been worse. "The frontiers in those parts have been greatly alarmed of late by a number of Tories who have banded together, threatening vengeance to all who have taken the oath of allegiance to the states," Carothers said in an April 24 letter to Pennsylvania authorities at York.

An express messenger from Kishacoquillas (present-day Lewistown) had just arrived at Carlisle with an urgent request for arms. The messenger reported that Colonel McLevy of Bedford County had recently come to the Kishacoquillas settlements "with an account that a body of Tories, near 320, in and above Standing Stone, had collected themselves together and drove a number of the inhabitants from Standing Stone Town (modern Huntingdon)."

The danger didn't daunt Roberdeau, who pressed on to Standing Stone, less than 20 miles short of the mine, and did some fact-finding. Writing from Standing Stone on April 23, he said he had determined that the situation was not as dire as the Bedford officer had said. "The insurgents (Tories) from this neighborhood, I am informed, are about thirty, one of them . . . has been taken and confession extorted, from which it appears that this banditti expect to be joined by 300 men from the other side the Allegheny. Reports more vague mention 1,000 whites and savages. . . . I have been informed by the most credible in this neighborhood that strangers, supposed to be from

Detroit, have been this winter among the disaffected inhabitants . . ." The late winter murders of western Pennsylvania settlers had been the work of Indian "savages set on by the governor of Detroit," Roberdeau said later.

Detroit was then considered part of British Canada, and the governor there—lieutenant governor, actually—was Henry Hamilton, a military officer notorious across the frontier for encouraging his Indian allies to take many American scalps.

By late April, Roberdeau had reached the mine, directed the soldiers to begin building a log fort as a protection against Indian raids, and decided to build a smelting furnace so the men could extract lead from the ore.

"I am happy to inform you that a very late discovery of a new vein promises the most ample supply, but I am very deficient in workmen," Roberdeau wrote on April 27. "Mr. Glen is with me to direct the making and burning of bricks, and is to come up to build a furnace, by which time I expect to be in such forwardness as to afford an ample supply to the army."

Details of how much lead the mine yielded are difficult to find. Available information suggests that the output was relatively small. It is known that Roberdeau's men used packhorses to carry lead ingots from the mine to present-day Water Street on the Juniata, where the ingots were transferred to dugout canoes and shipped downriver in small convoys, first to the Susquehanna River and then south about 25 miles to Middletown. Soldiers accompanied these convoys to guard against ambushes.

The remoteness of the mine and fort made them difficult to supply, but John Harris, a merchant at Paxton (present-day Harrisburg) willingly took on the task. Spring rains had brought high water to both the Susquehanna and Juniata, and Harris wanted to take advantage of it "as perhaps no other may happen till next fall." Harris was alluding to the hazards of shipping by water when summer dry spells caused river levels to fall. Navigating a heavily laden boat in low water increased the risk of running onto large rocks.

"I am as good a judge of the navigation, in either boat or canoe, on our river as can be found," Harris said in a June 3 letter to George Bryan, vice president of the Pennsylvania executive council, then meeting in Lancaster. "I expect to send up a quantity of stores to the lead mines, up Juniata, at Water Street, as soon as I receive a letter from Mr. Roberdeau, which I hourly expect."

Made into bullets, the lead from Sinking Valley slowly made its way into the hands of the soldiers. Even so, Colonel Samuel Hunter, the commander at Fort Augusta (present-day Sunbury) noted in a letter dated May 30, 1778: "the quantity of powder and lead allotted for (Northumberland) County is but very small, considering what number (of men) is able to bear arms, suppose we are not quite out of ammunition, yet it's not when it's wanted that we should have to send for it."

It appears that the mine was active for only a year or two. In April 1779, Joseph Reed, recommended the construction of a storage magazine at "the lead mine in Sinking Valley."

Tories, Terror, and Tea

Top:
The exterior wall of one of reconstructed Fort Roberdeau's bastions.

Right:
A swivel gun inside Fort Roberdeau is aimed toward the front gate for use if any enemies get through the main entrance. (The author poses with the gun.)

Below:
The interior of Fort Roberdeau

In late May, William Holliday, one of the founders of Hollidaysburg, reported, "There is a quantity of lead at the mines in this county," but that was hardly the case at Fort Augusta, less than a hundred miles to the east. Soldiers sent out from Fort Augusta regularly patrolled forest paths also used by hostile warriors even though Colonel Hunter reported, "we are scarce of ammunition, especially lead. There is none."

Sometimes, frontiersmen who lived near Fort Roberdeau walked to the mine to obtain small quantities of lead. Consider the case of William Moore, whose homestead was near the Adam Holliday farm. As related by Rupp, the Pennsylvania historian:

> Early one morning, Moore, accompanied by a boy named M'Cartney, set out for the mine on foot. "As he was passing a log by the side of the road, with some brush behind it, a shot from an Indian in ambush caused him to jump several feet into the air; and he started off into the bushes, in a direction opposite to that which he should naturally have taken . . .
>
> "The boy and the Indian at once jumped behind trees; but the latter peeping out from his tree, which was not large, the boy availed himself of the chance to put a bullet into his buttock, which was exposed at the other side.
>
> "The Indian ran, and dropped his belt and knife; and the road was found strewed with bunches of bloody leaves, with which he had attempted to stanch the wound. But the man himself was not found."

When M'Cartney returned alone to the Moore settlement for help, Moore's brother Daniel rounded up a rescue party, found William, and brought him home unharmed.

CHAPTER NINE

1778

Tories, War Parties Terrorize Susquehanna Settlements

Border warfare had its own seasonal rules during the Revolutionary War. These included a notion that the deeper the snow blanket, the fewer the hostile incursions. Militia commanders knew that deep winter snowfalls provided a measure of safety for the residents of Frontier Pennsylvania. If Pennsylvanians were snowed in, so were the British and their native allies at the nearest enemy outposts—Forts Niagara and Detroit. As spring came on, with longer days and warmer temperatures, the commandant at Fort Augusta at the Forks of the Susquehanna River kept a nervous eye on the region's melting snow cover. "In case the Indians has [sic] any intention of committing hostilities, it will be very soon now, as the snow is partly all gone," Colonel Samuel Hunter wrote on March 28.

The colonel had another major worry: the lack of weapons and ammunitions available to the militia soldiers under his command as well as in the garrisons of the outposts for which he was responsible. Hunter articulated this worry quite plainly. As he told Wharton, the president of Pennsylvania, "When I was down last winter, I endeavored . . . to purchase some good guns, but could get none that was worth buying. Only two rifles, and them with sixty ordinary muskets we had made for this county, is all the public arms amongst us. I am getting all the arms that's worth repairing put in order."

Conditions had hardly improved six weeks later when Hunter sent another report to Wharton, this one dated May 14: "We are scarce of guns, not more than one half of the militia is provided with arms, and a number of them very ordinary. Our powder is exceeding bad, and not fit for rifles in any shape. And as for flints we can get none to buy."

Another concern: the Indian raids had resumed. Not surprisingly, first they attacked homesteads along Bald Eagle Creek (near modern Lock Haven) and within the 20-mile-long Penns Valley that extended from Woodward southwest to Centre Hall. "I received two expresses last Monday," he said, "one from Bald Eagle settlement, informing me that the Indians had killed one man there . . ., the other from Penn's Valley, informing me that they had killed and scalped one Jacob Stanford, his wife and two childer (children)."

Hunter ordered militia soldiers "to march into Penn's Valley, . . . to scout along the frontiers . . . (to march) up towards the Great Island (opposite Lock Haven, and) to cover the frontiers there."

In addition to hostile Indians and inadequate firearms, the soldiers experienced a "want of provisions. As for meat, there is very little to be had in this county and that very dear," the colonel said. The price for bacon and flour had shot up dramatically.

Every May and June, immense quantities of American shad swam up the Susquehanna to spawn, and Hunter sought to take advantage of this. "I have ordered some people that lives nigh the Great Island to preserve shad and barrel them up for the use of the militia that will be stationed there this summer," he told Wharton.

The West Branch settlements in a region that includes the modern communities of Lock Haven, Jersey Shore and Williamsport were subject to repeated raids. With frequent "expresses coming to inform me of savages killing and captivating the back inhabitants," the colonel had much more to report twelve days later:

Near the mouth of Bald Eagle Creek (Lock Haven), on May 16, a war party killed and scalped three farmers "putting in a spring crop." Near Pine Creek (Jersey Shore) two days later, Indians abducted a man, woman and child. Two days after that, they attacked a house near Lycoming Creek (Williamsport) where there were two men and seven women and children.

"They took them all prisoners," Hunter said in a May 26 report. "And yesterday there was an express from Muncy, informing me of three families, consisting of sixteen in number, being killed and taken away from Loyalsock (also Williamsport)." Rescue parties found only two bodies and advised Hunter that "the enemy had set fire to the houses."

The raids have "so alarmed the inhabitants ... that they are all fled to Samuel Wallis's, where they intend to make a stand," Hunter said.

Wallis had been a shipping merchant in Philadelphia merchant before becoming a surveyor and moving to the Susquehanna Valley in the late 1760s. He acquired vast holdings of land in the West Branch Valley and in 1769 built a two-story stone house between present-day Muncy and Williamsport. It stood on high ground near a bend in the river.

The homesteaders who sought refuge at Wallis's plantation included John and Judah Thomson, a husband and wife from New Jersey, and their son, a toddler also named John. As the days passed without any indication of Indian war parties in the region, John decided to return to his farm, which was about seven miles to the west, if only to see what had happened to it during his absence. His friend, Peter Shufelt, went along, as did a sixteen-year-old boy, William Wyckoff.

That was on Thursday, June 9. The same day, two officers—Colonel Hosterman and Captain Reynolds—left Wallis's, headed west along the Great Shamokin Path with a detachment of 13 men. They were transporting a shipment of ammunition for two forts higher up the West Branch: Antes Fort (opposite present-day Jersey Shore) and Fort Reid (at modern Lock Haven).

As the colonel reported afterwards, "when they had got as far as Loyal Sock (Creek) ... and had just crossed the creek, they heard a firing and yells. They judged it to be three-quarters of a mile up the creek, (and) they pushed on to the firing as fast as they could."

But the Indians were gone. The soldiers proceeded to Thomson's farm "about a mile from the place they first heard the firing. . . . They found the barn on fire (it contained grain in the sheaf)," the colonel said. But the cabin hadn't been disturbed. "They found Thomson's powder horn, with a bullet hole through it, near the house; saw several moccasin and shoe tracks, but could not find Thomson, Shufelt, or Wyckoff . . ."

On Friday, June 10, the soldiers and refugees at Wallis's "grew uneasy and sent off a party between 20 and 30 under Captain Shaffer." When they reached the Thomson homestead, they "examined it and all about, (and) at length found him and Shufelt [in] . . . a field among some pine grubs. Thomson was shot through the left side and through the powder horn and scalped. Shufelt was shot through the left shoulder and scalped. They lay but a little distance apart," Hosterman reported. He noted that the Indians "were so near Thompson when they shot him that his jacket was burned."

Wyckoff was taken north to Indian country as a prisoner, but was eventually exchanged and returned to the Susquehanna Valley.

Thomson's widow and son made their way down the West Branch to Fort Augusta, and soon after walked back to New Jersey. They never came back to the West Branch.

The British, by evacuating Philadelphia and returning to New York in late spring of 1778,

Tories, Terror, and Tea

Inside the walls of Fort Augusta. Photo shows a detail of an outdoor model built by the Northumberland County Historical Society on the original fort site in Sunbury, Pennsylvania. The buildings are replicas of barracks that housed soldiers during the American Revolutionary War.

would inadvertently ease the shortage of firearms at Fort Augusta, George Bryan, vice president of the Executive Council, advised Hunter in a May 29 letter. "As it is expected that the British army will in a few days abandon our state, the public arms in the hands of the militia in the eastern counties will be no longer needed for the service on the Delaware," Bryan said. He suggested that these weapons could well be sent out to the Susquehanna, "but these are not rifles."

Bryan also advised that the state had ordered firearms and ammunition to be shipped to Fort Augusta: "70 rifle guns sent from this place (Lancaster), 31 rifles, and 69 muskets ordered from Northampton." Also, the state's Board of War was providing "one ton of lead, half a ton of

Pointed logs above a dry moat create obstacles for would-be attackers of Fort Augusta at Sunbury, Pennsylvania. Photo shows a detail of an outdoor model built by the Northumberland County Historical Society on the original fort site. The buildings are replicas of barracks that housed soldiers during the American Revolutionary War.

gunpowder, and 2,000 flints . . . for the use of the frontiers." Of these, "one fourth part was allotted to you."

The official added that Continental troops would soon come to the aid of Pennsylvania's frontier settlements. "The 8th Pennsylvania Regiment is actually marched from camp . . .," Bryan said, disclosing that one "officer tells me that he means to enter the Indian Country and attack them at home."

While Bryan tried to encourage the colonel, events along the upper Susquehanna pushed in the opposite direction. Indeed, the attacks intensified throughout June. "We are really in a melancholy situation," Hunter advised John Hambright, a Northumberland County representative on the Executive Council. "The back inhabitants has all evacuated their habitations and assembled in different places. . . . What a panic prevails in this county. It is really distressing to see the inhabitants flying away and leaving their all, especially the Jersey people that came up here this last winter and spring. Not one stays, but sets off to the Jerseys again."

On June 30, a large force of Loyalist militia and pro-British Indians invaded the Wyoming Valley along the North Branch. Their objective: destruction of the forts, farms and villages that settlers from Connecticut had established in the region during the past dozen years. (A 1662 land grant by King Charles II of England had given the region to Connecticut, which officially recognized it as Westmoreland.)

"I arrived with about 500 rangers and Indians at Wyoming, and encamped on an eminence which overlooks the greatest part of the settlement . . .," said Major John Butler, a Tory officer whose militia force was known as Butler's Rangers. Accompanied by as many of 600 Indians, the invaders included Sir John Johnson's Royal Greens, as well as a large number of Tories from settlements in Pennsylvania, New Jersey and New York.

"Two Loyalists who came into my camp informed me that the rebels could muster about 800 men who were all assembled in their forts," Butler reported in a July 8 letter.

On the afternoon of July 3, a force of 400 to 500 Connecticut men marched out onto the plain

Wyoming Valley Massacre

on the river's west bank at present-day Wyoming to repel them. "When they were within 200 yards of us they began firing," Butler said.

The Indians and the Tories returned fire and soon routed the Wyoming men. Butler said his men took only five prisoners, but 227 scalps.

The next day, one of the leaders of the Connecticut settlers—Colonel Nathan Denison—met with Butler and arranged to capitulate. Denison "assures me that they have lost one colonel, two majors, seven captains, thirteen lieutenants, eleven ensigns, and two hundred and sixty eight privates. On our side are killed one Indian; two Rangers and eight Indians wounded," Butler said.

The major allowed the civilians to depart, then torched the valley. "In this incursion we have taken and destroyed eight palisaded forts and burned about 1,000 dwelling homes, all their mills, etc.," he said in his July 8 report. "We have also killed and drove off about 1,000 head of horned cattle, and sheep and swine in great numbers."

As news spread of the Tory victory over the Wyoming Valley, panic swept throughout the Susquehanna River Valley.

"Both branches are almost evacuated, and from all appearances the towns of Northumberland and Sunbury will be the frontier in less than twenty-four hours," Colonel Hunter wrote on July 9. "The inhabitants of both towns, with a few of the fugitives from the upper parts of the county, seem determined to make a stand, but how long they can do it seems very precarious."

On Sunday, July 10, "the banks of the Susquehanna—from Middletown up to the Blue Mountain—were entirely clad with the inhabitants of Northumberland County, who had moved off, as well as many in the river in boats, canoes, and rafts etc.," reported Colonel Bartrem Galbraith, who headed the Lancaster County militia. "Indeed, the Inhabitants of Wiconisco Valley, which is about twenty-five miles above Harris's ferry, in this county, were moving on Sunday last, and that the people lower down were thinking to follow."

The evacuees included William Maclay, one of the founders of both Sunbury and Northumberland County. "I will not trouble you with a recital of the inconveniences I suffered while I brought my family by water to this place," Maclay said. "I never in my life saw such scenes of distress. The river and the roads leading down it were covered with men, women and children, flying for their lives, many without any property at all . . ."

In a July 12 letter to the Pennsylvania Executive Council, Maclay wrote: "For God's Sake, for the sake of the country, let Colonel Hunter be reinforced at Sunbury. Send him but a single company, if you cannot do more. Mrs. Hunter came down with me. As he is now disencumbered of his family, I am convinced he will do every thing that can be expected from a brave and determined man."

Settlers had become so terrified that "the appearance of half a dozen Indians in that neighborhood would have struck a panic through the confused multitude," Samuel Wallis said from his plantation along the West Branch.

Writing to Colonel Timothy Matlack, secretary of the Executive Council of Pennsylvania on July 24, Wallis declared that "unless . . . Continental Troops can be stationed amongst us," the upper Susquehanna region "will be evacuated in a very short time."

Wallis contended that homesteaders throughout the valley had largely lost confidence in militia soldiers: "It will be in vain to amuse the people with saying a single word to them about the militia, unless some continental troops are mixed with them."

Panic had escalated into terror.

CHAPTER TEN

1778

Captured Settler Forced to Live Like an Indian

Much of northeastern Pennsylvania once belonged to Connecticut—or so many people in Connecticut thought. They believed that, in a formal grant in 1662, King Charles II of England had given this land to Connecticut when it was organized as a royal colony.

A century later—during the 1760s and the early 1770s—hundreds of Connecticut people headed west across the Hudson River, which coursed through colonial New York, and settled along the Susquehanna River's North Branch. Some of the newcomers emigrated from Rhode Island as well. By 1777, an estimated population of 2,600 New Englanders had taken up residence along the North Branch, and their settlements had become part of a new county that Connecticut created—Westmoreland.

One of these settlers was a middle-aged man named Luke Swetland. Born in the Connecticut village of Lebanon in 1729, Swetland and his wife

Hannah moved to the Susquehanna's Wyoming Valley during the 1760s. When the American Revolution began, Swetland sided with the Whigs, or Patriots, who in 1776 declared the United States independent of Britain.

To be sure, not all North Branch settlers favored rebellion. More than a few of the more conservative were Loyalists, or Tories, who opposed what was then termed "Independency." As the dispute between crown and rebellious colonists began to turn violent, many Wyoming Valley Tories moved higher up the Susquehanna Valley.

When war broke out, there were enough adult males living in Westmoreland to organize a military unit, the 24th Regiment of Connecticut. It consisted of two companies. Swetland enlisted in Captain Robert Durkee's company. In December 1776, the Continental Congress ordered both companies "to join General Washington, with all possible expedition."

The Wyoming Valley soldiers marched more than a hundred miles to the east, reaching the American positions in New Jersey in time to take part in a January 20, 1777, battle along the Millstone River near present-day Manville. There a force of 450 New Jersey militia and the two Westmoreland regiments routed 500 British and Hessian regulars who were guarding a foraging party engaged in plundering a mill owned by Abraham Van Nest along the Millstone. The British fled, leaving behind 49 horse-drawn wagons that they had loaded with flour and other supplies. The victorious Americans took the wagons

20 miles north to Washington's new camp near Morristown.

The Westmorelanders also took part in the 1777 battles of Bound Brook in northern New Jersey, and Brandywine and Germantown in southeastern Pennsylvania. They also went into winter camp at Valley Forge, about twenty miles northeast of Philadelphia. Swetland was discharged in early January 1778 and walked the 100-mile distance home to the Wyoming Valley.

As the year 1778 progressed, rumors circulated that the British at Fort Niagara on Lake Ontario planned to send their Indian allies against American settlements along the upper Susquehanna. Concerned that Westmoreland homes remained largely unprotected, other Wyoming Valley soldiers left Valley Forge as well. By May, so many Westmoreland men had resigned that the two Connecticut companies had to be consolidated.

Fighting broke out along the upper Susquehanna in late May, and warfare intensified in early July when a large force of British and Indians invaded the Wyoming Valley.

Although Swetland was a combat veteran, he stayed behind when the Wyoming defenders marched out to meet Major John Butler's invasion force on July 3. He was one of four men selected by lot to remain as guards for the women, children and elderly who sought refuge at the fort called Forty Fort on the river's west bank.

The Tories and Indians carried the day. In the aftermath of a battle known in American history as the Wyoming Massacre, the Indian raiders went through the valley, "burning buildings, killing and driving off our cattle, sheep, horses and hogs, and plundering every thing they could find," Swetland wrote later.

Discouraged and fearful, many of Swetland's neighbors immediately left the region, but Swetland, then 49, and his wife Hannah decided to stay on their land, along with their four sons, "the oldest of them about fourteen years old," he said.

Just 10 days after the battle, they decided on temporary flight after "two or three Indians came and told us that the Indians were returning with some wild Indians that had not been with them in the battle nor plundering, and if we were not all gone in the space of two hours we should all be scalped."

The Swetlands left quickly, and walked the nearly 50 miles to Fort Penn at present-day Stroudsburg. They found sanctuary there and remained "until a party of Continental soldiers, together with a number of the Susquehanna inhabitants, were going back to retake the place and also to harvest the grain. I went with them," Swetland said. Returning to his farm, Swetland harvested his grain "and thrashed some."

There were few mills remaining in the valley so he and another farmer, Joseph Blanchard, gathered up small quantities of grain and "went down the Susquehanna river in a canoe about eight miles below Wilksbury (Wilkes-Barre) fort," he said.

Not far from present-day Nanticoke, a flour mill was running alongside a creek a good half-mile up from the river. Blanchard and Swetland beached their canoe and set off for the mill. "Having carried our wheat to the mill and got it floured, I borrowed the miller's horse to carry my flour to the canoe. Blanchard had his flour on his back and when we had got within a few rods (30 to 50 feet) of the canoe, six Indians were hid under the weeds and bushes close by the path and when we came against them they started up within about two or three steps of us and said 'Howdy.' . . . They took hold of us in an instant. we not having opportunity to run or scarce time to think surrendered without making any resistance," Swetland wrote.

The war party soon headed north with the two prisoners. As Swetland recalled later:

"We went about ten miles that night and made a halt, struck up a fire, and they laid us on our backs, pinioned our arms behind us, tied round the neck and middle with rope and tied together, one of the Indians lay on the rope between us. This as I remember was on Monday, August 24, 1778."

The warriors and captives broke camp before sunrise the next morning, heading north toward Iroquois country. One man told Swetland that "he was my master, and drove me before him . . . and would often strike me with his tomahawk on my hips and sides, sometimes on one side and say, 'Tullaway,' then on the other side and say, 'God damn Tullaway,' and then would laugh."

If he knew it, Swetland didn't explain the meaning of the Tullaway phrase or why it caused the warrior to laugh, but the repeated beatings injured his sides and hips. "My feet were also bruised and sore, for they made me throw away my shoes and gave me deerskin moccasins. . . . Being forced to run where the ground was stony made stone bruises on the bottoms of my feet," he said.

They had traveled nearly forty miles by the end of the third day, Wednesday, August 26. "Sometime in the evening we came to Meshoppen (along the North Branch), where the Tories had an encampment," Swetland said. "I was well acquainted with some of them. They said they were glad we were taken, but sorry we were not killed; however, they gave us victuals. This night we were tied to a spar (pole) of their hut, and two of the Tories stood sentry over us all night, and the Tories, both men and women, danced round us the most part of the night.

"Next morning my old neighbors the Tories appeared friendly, gave me a razor and soap to shave myself with, and gave more victuals to me, and told the Indians that I was an honest man."

This comment served to soften the warriors' attitude toward Swetland. "The Indian captain took me to himself and was very tender of me," the prisoner said later. "He found I was very lame. He opened the stone bruises on my feet and showed all the favor he could to me. We went on slowly that day up the river, found several Tory families where we had good usage."

"The next day (Thursday, August 27) we came to Tioga (present-day Athens, about 45 miles farther north) where was another camp of my neighbor Tories and some Indians. The Tories spoke roughly to me, but gave us buttermilk to drink.

When we set off from there my Indian master went along a little before me and I, being lame, went very slowly . . ."

As Swetland walked, he suddenly suffered a hard blow to the "side of my head, which nearly brought me to the ground, I looked and saw it was an Indian that followed me from the Tory camp. I did my best to get out of his way, but he followed me sometime with kicks and blows till at last he went back to his camp. . . . My master stopped till I came up and then made me go before him."

It was "very dark" and "quite late in the evening" when the war party reached the Indian town of Chemung, less than 20 miles to the west. The captain gave the prisoner halloo which Swetland said "rallied the whole town, numbers of them met us yelling and screaming, jumping and running. The Indian captain took hold of my hand, (and) ran with me some distance into a house, so they did not hurt me."

But Blanchard had no such luck. The Indians "took Blanchard and very much abused him, but after some time he came where I was, being wounded on the head and face. (He) was very bloody. The captain appeared pitiful (and) gave him water to wash his bloody face and head. Here we lay that night, not bound at all."

The next day (Friday, August 28), the Indians separated Swetland and Blanchard. "My companion took his leave of me," Swetland reported. "He said. 'I shall never see you again. Pray for me. It is all we can do for each other."

During the next several days, the Indians took Swetland farther north still to an Iroquois town along the east side of Seneca Lake. It had 20 log houses and an orchard with apple and peach trees. Living there was an old woman "to whom I was given as a grandson," Swetland said. Some time after this the war captain came by to visit. The man "told me this old squaw is your grandmother, and pointing (to) the biggest of the little ones said, 'That is your sister, and the two little ones are your cousins,' and so went on through the town telling me who were my relations, and said I should soon be an Indian and then I should know all about it."

Appletown quickly became the captive's new home. "Here I lived twelve months and two days," he wrote. ". . . The Indians were remarkably kind . . . (and) made me many fine presents, I had from one and another three hats, five blankets, near twenty pipes, six razors, six knives, several spoons, gun and ammunition, fireworks, several Indian pockets, one Indian razor, awls, needles, goose-quills, paper and many other things of small value."

Meanwhile, back in the Wyoming Valley, 150 miles to the south, Swetland's family gave him up for dead and returned to Connecticut.

CHAPTER ELEVEN

1782

Indians, British Rangers Burn Frontier Town in Western Pa.

Largely forgotten, a 1782 Indian raid destroyed a thriving frontier settlement whose taverns served soldiers, Indian traders and other travelers along the Forbes Road in Western Pennsylvania.

General John Forbes built that road in 1758 during the French and Indian War as the British army marched the 175 miles from Carlisle to present-day Pittsburgh to force the evacuation of Fort DuQuesne, a French post built in 1754. Forbes succeeded in ousting the French, and his soldiers subsequently built Fort Pitt on the site of DuQuesne.

After the war, the road became a key highway for land-hungry settlers from the east, among them a York County man named Robert Hanna.

Hanna established a homestead along the road about 35 miles east of Pittsburgh. He operated a tavern, and laid out lots for a new village, which he called Hanna's Town. The settlement proved popular with travelers, who found few other amenities on the trek through the forests and over the Allegheny Mountains.

In 1773, when Pennsylvania's colonial government created Westmoreland County, the village became the county seat. At first, court was held in Hanna's tavern, but eventually it moved to a two-story log courthouse erected nearby. Another two-story log structure served as the county jail.

During the Revolutionary War, Western Pennsylvania saw much fighting between American soldiers and British rangers and their Indian allies. At some point, the settlers at Hannastown erected a log stockade at the edge of town. The stockade consisted of pickets, or upright logs firmly anchored in the ground. It guarded a spring and featured a blockhouse.

By 1782, Hannastown consisted of the jail, the courthouse, the stockade, Robert Hanna's tavern and nearly 30 other buildings.

On Saturday, July 13, 1782, many Hannastown men went north of the village to help Michael Huffnagle harvest wheat on his farm. In mid-day, a worker spotted an Indian war party heading their way so the harvesters rushed to the village and spread the alarm. By the time the raiders reached Hannastown, the villagers were inside their stockade, its gate closed.

"The people of this place behaved brave," Huffnagle wrote less than a week later. They retired to the safety of the fort, even though doing so left all their homes and

Historic marker near Hannastown

The pillory at Historic Hanna's Town, a reconstructed village that occupies the site of the original settlement of Hannastown in southwestern Pennsylvania.

possessions "a prey to the enemy, and with 20 men only, and nine guns in good order, we stood the attack till dark."

The fighting began in the afternoon at about 2 o'clock. "At first, some of the enemy came close to the pickets (in the stockade wall), but were soon obliged to retire farther off. I cannot inform you what number of the enemy may be killed, as we see them from the fort carrying off several," Huffnagle said.

Huffnagle estimated that the raiding party consisted of about 100 Indians and British. After the raiders left, "we found several jackets, the buttons marked with the king's 8th Regiment," he said.

When news of the raid reached Pittsburgh, a settler named Ephraim Douglass gathered information about the attack and passed it on to

In July 1782, a raiding party of British and Indians burned the western Pennsylvania settlement of Hannastown. These buildings are part of Historic Hanna's Town, a reconstructed village that occupies the site of the original village.

Pennsylvania officials in Philadelphia. With the villagers inside the fort, the raiders took over the buildings outside it, "from whence they kept a continual fire upon the fort . . . till night, without doing any other damage than wounding one little girl within the walls," Douglass reported.

As they departed, "they carried away a great number of horses and everything of value in the deserted houses, destroyed all the cattle, hogs, and poultry within their reach, and burned all the houses in the village except two." He explained that the raiders had torched these structures, but the fire failed to destroy them.

As General William Irvine, then headquartered at Fort Pitt, later told George Washington, a force of British soldiers, together with 500 Indian warriors, had left western New York State earlier in 1782, intending to attack Fort Pitt. Finding the fort too strong, the British "contented themselves . . . by sending small parties on the frontier, one of which burned Hannastown," Irvine said.

Although the villagers survived the attack, they lost their homes and possessions, so most left and never came back. Some few returned to rebuild, but Hannastown never recovered. In time, the main road was realigned with the new routing taking it several miles to the south. The county seat eventually also was moved south to nearby Greensburg.

Today, a reconstructed village, known as Historic Hanna's Town, occupies the site. It is maintained by the Westmoreland County Historical Society and Westmoreland County Parks and Recreation.

CHAPTER TWELVE

1782

'Hijacker Pointed Pistol, Said He'd Blow My Brains Out'

———•◆•———

A paying passenger, Philadelphian Thomas Bedwell rode most of the day on Friday, July 26, 1782, in John Johnston's covered freight wagon on the old Lancaster-Philadelphia Road. The wagon was bound for Lancaster and then on to York. It was followed by a second wagon belonging to Archibald Henderson, teamster and friend of Johnston.

Bedwell had left Philadelphia late the previous afternoon, and, tired from two days of being jostled and bumped, he decided to stretch his legs and walk for a spell. So he got out and started to do just that.

It was late afternoon—between 5 and 6 o'clock. Twilight was still several hours away since it was mid-summer, and Bedwell soon walked far ahead of Johnston's wagon. He was just west of present-day Coatesville, and upon reaching the top of Valley Hill he glanced back to see the wagon and Henderson's wagon a short distance behind it.

Bedwell said later that he was about 100 yards in front of Johnston's wagon when he "saw two men sitting on a log by the road side with their heads down resting on their hands." He paid little attention to them, and walked past them, his mind elsewhere.

Suddenly Bedwell heard running feet and realized the men were "running after him." They told him to stop, and he did. As they came up to him, the strangers displayed "some large pistols with brass barrels," Bedwell said.

Bedwell realized quickly that they had disguised themselves by blackening their faces and powdering their hair. That explained why they'd had their heads down as he'd passed. The tall man wore a cocked hat, and the short man's nose much resembled a hawk's beak.

The gunmen took Bedwell into the woods, tied his hands behind him, and quickly "put him up against a tree and interrogated him as to the loading of the wagons, particularly as to what money was in them."

Bedwell explained that he was merely a passenger and didn't know what kind of cargo the wagons were hauling. "He (Bedwell) had told them that Mr. Johnston had some money of his to keep for him. They said they belonged to a larger gang and wanted nothing but public property and would return all private property again or would not touch it."

Bedwell's interrogation took a very short time, and the robbers ordered him to stay where he was before they hurried back to the road. Upon leaving, "they . . . charged him to continue there on pain of being shot."

By now the Johnston and Henderson wagons were cresting the hill.

Archibald Henderson had walked alongside his wagon as it came up the hill. As it reached the brow, one of the two strangers suddenly walked up to his team, startling him. He "came and took my horse by the head and led him towards the woods. I ran up and asked him where he was going with the horses. He pointed a pistol towards me and said if I would say a word he would blow my brains out."

The second teamster, John Johnston, reported that immediately after "one of the men seized Mr. Henderson's leading horse, the other . . . presented two pistols at my breast. They were large pistols with brass barrels. He had two other smaller pistols at his belt."

The second hijacker ordered Johnston to "follow the other wagon immediately and said if I offered to stop or fasten upon any tree designedly he would blow my brains out. He took us down about a quarter of a mile from the road to a small valley, where there was about an acre of ground or some small piece cleared."

Johnston added that "one of the men came up to me and presented his pistols and ordered the other one to tie my hands behind my back. When I was tied, I looked round and saw Mr. Bedwell there tied. Mr. Bedwell was a passenger in my wagon from Philadelphia."

Henderson's load consisted of "a hogshead of clothing, four barrels of vinegar and a bale of blankets belonging to the public, and had in my wagon some sugar and coffee and some small articles of private property."

By "public," Henderson meant it belonged to the Continental Congress or the Continental Army.

Johnston's wagon was "loaded with goods for Mr. Swope, Mr. Hay and Mr. Billmeyer of Yorktown." Yorktown was an early name for present-day York.

Jacob Miller, a passenger in Henderson's wagon, had been asleep when the hijackers appeared. "The wagon turned off the road and seemed as if it would overset, which awakened me," Miller said later. "I jumped up and looked out; saw a fellow with his face blackened having hold of the horses. The fellow when he saw me came to me and presented two pistols to me, and said he would blow my brains out if I stirred a step."

Johnston said that when the wagons reached the clearing, the robbers ordered Jacob Miller to start unloading the Henderson wagon. The larger man "left the other . . . as a guard over us and went to the road again. Shortly after I heard a pistol go off. Shortly after he brought a Major (John) Beaton of Chester County to the place where we was [sic] and tied his hands behind him and ordered him to sit down."

The smaller robber "pulled off the end gate from the tail of my wagon," then "told me to throw out the blanketing. Before I had time to get on my wagon he said to Jacob Miller, who was still in it, 'You big son of a bitch, throw them out.' Miller then rolled out the bale of blankets."

The robbers inspected the blankets and realized that they were destined for soldiers in the Continental Army. "They then ordered the vinegar barrels to be rolled out. We rolled one out that did not break. The tall man then got a stone and knocked in the head of it."

The other vinegar barrels were also "rolled out and stove except one which remained," Johnston said. "They then ordered the hogshead of clothing to be rolled out. It did not break. The little man with a stone knocked the hoops off and knocked the head out. They took part of the clothing out and throwed [sic] them in a heap. They said, 'These will do us no good, and as they belong to the Continental (soldiers) we will burn them.' They then went from my wagon to Johnston's wagon."

As the robbers rummaged through Johnston's wagon, they found a parcel containing lead. "This is to kill the Indians," the smaller bandit said.

"He then took up a keg," Johnston said later. "'This,' says he, 'is powder to go with the lead and threw the keg from him as far as he could." The head came off the keg, revealing that it contained tea, not gunpowder.

"Damn the odds," one robber said as he examined the tea. "This is what began the war."

Johnston was hauling boxes that Philadelphia merchants were shipping to customers in York. The names of the customers had been written on the box tops.

"They then examined the boxes and found Mr. Swope's and Mr. Hay's name on them and said they knew them to be damned rebels and knocked them open. When they had them open and saw that the goods suited them, the little man took a parcel and carried them to the left of where we were." The hijacker came back presently "and took another armful and filled his pockets with snuff boxes, tapes and other small articles and carried them to the right of where we were. Then he returned and took another armful and pocketful and went to the left of us again," Johnston said.

At one point, the hijackers started a fire. Bedwell said they had found an assortment of wooden broom handles, "which they called flag staffs," in one of the wagons, and decided to burn them. They emptied a large hogshead and discovered that it was "filled with soldiers coats, blue faced with white, the buttons marked U. S.," Johnston said. Added Bedwell: "They burnt all the clothing, saying it was a high satisfaction for them to burn it, as it was for the damned rebels and wished they had a great deal more of it," Bedwell said.

Henderson said that the smaller man tossed "the coats on it, saying he knew the soldiers had need for them, but it made no odds as they were damned rebels."

Henderson added: "They then rummaged the boxes from Johnston's wagon again and finding a parcel of handkerchiefs with 'General Washington' stamped on them, they kicked them about, saying they would burn the damned son of a bitch, too, if they had him. They put the handkerchiefs then into a bag."

Suddenly, the hijackers "heard three other wagons go along the road and lamented that we were not sufficiently secured to enable them to take the other three wagons," Bedwell said.

While all this was going on, Henderson said that "the big man . . . guarded us with two pistols.

The little fellow . . . asked us if we were not dry, and took us one by one to a spring to drink.

"About this time an old man who was gathering herbs appeared just at the edge of the cleared place. The big man ran to him and told him to stand and brought him and placed him with us."

The robbers then began to fill two bags with goods out of a chest from Mr. Johnston's wagon. . . . Any thing they did not choose to take they kicked away. While they were filling the bags, the big man went towards the spring. I at that time saw a man on a sorrel horse a few rods from the spring, and the big man talking to him. I could not hear what they said, and do not know the man who was on horseback. He had a long Quaker-like coat on, buttoned, and a round hat, and was without a saddle. The man on horseback went away, and the big man returned.

Throughout the ordeal Bedwell clearly had ample time to study the hijackers, and afterwards provided the authorities with detailed descriptions:

He said later that he thought he had seen one man in Philadelphia. "One of them was a light, made-well proportioned man, with brown hair cut short. (He) had on a large French cocked hat, a dyed fustian olive colored coat or frock with outside pockets, . . . corduroy velvet breeches of nearly the same color; had a plain pair of silver buttons in his sleeves of an oval form (and) had a small silver broach in his bosom set in diamonds."

The robbers' exertions in taking the wagons had caused them to perspire, and the sweat had washed the black off their faces. Bedwell saw that he was "a ruddy complexioned person with a thin nose and thin lips and rather sour countenance. The other was a tall, well-set man, dressed in a linen coat, jacket and overalls, which were tied round the small of the leg; had brown hair tied behind (and) a pale complexion with an aquiline nose."

Added Jacob Miller, the passenger who had been sleeping in Henderson's wagon: "The little man had four pistols in his belt and two in his hands, and the big man had four pistols that I saw. They damned us for rebels."

It was nearly dark by the time the robbers decided that they had put enough plunder in their sacks. As they prepared to leave, "they came to us and told us not to describe them and that if we did they would catch us going up and down the road," Henderson said. "They went away then and took the bags with them. I heard one of them say that he had rode up the road with a Continental officer, who had told him of the wagons and their loading."

"We were there about three hours," said Johnston. "It was night before they went away."

Early on Johnston had told the big man "that I hoped they would not take any thing about ourselves. He said by no means."

Despite the assurance, after a while, "the little fellow . . . came to me and asked me for my money," Johnston said. "I gave it to him tied in a linen purse. He went away with it on pretense to get a drink. When they were going away, I spoke to the big one and said that he had promised that nothing should be taken from myself. He then ordered the little one to return my money. He returned me my purse and I found upon examination that there was £7 15 5 gone out of it. It was all my own money."

When the teamsters saw the hijackers getting ready to leave, "We asked them if they would untie us before they went away," Johnston said. ". . . They untied me and left the major and Mr. Bedwell tied. Neither Mr. Henderson nor Jacob Miller were tied during the whole transaction."

The robbers wanted plenty of time for their getaway. As they rode off, "they . . . charged us not to move from the place till a full quarter of an hour after they were gone on peril of our lives," Johnston said.

"I did not hear them call one another by their names," Johnston added. "They said one was captain one day, the other the next."

Bedwell provided other details: "Before they went away, they apologized to us for their treatment of us, saying they were friends to the king and his government, were in the country and were denied the means of getting out of it, and had no other way to support themselves."

Jacob Miller reported, "Before they went off, they took the saddle and bridle from Major Beaton's Horse and let him run, and told the major that he should not ride."

Despite the warnings of the robbers, the teamsters and their passengers salvaged some of the merchandise and got back on the road within ten minutes. They all wanted to report the holdup, so they made their way to a tavern that a magistrate, Squire William Clingan, operated along the road. But the magistrate wasn't at home, and Johnston and Henderson continued to Lancaster, 28 miles to the west. For his part, Major Beaton disappears from the record at this point. Presumably, he went to his home in Chester County.

The teamsters and their passengers reached Lancaster on Sunday, July 28, and went directly to see William Atlee, a lawyer who was deeply involved in civic and political affairs. Atlee questioned the men closely and took detailed statements from them.

Though none of the travelers knew the identities of the robbers, Atlee determined that people living near the area where the hijacking occurred had strong suspicions "against a certain Thomas Buller and one Pile, who are both of Chester county and (who) may be known to Major Beaton, who was attacked and made prisoner by them while they plundered the wagons, as he is an inhabitant of Chester County. I have not yet seen him to have his account of the transaction, but shall persist in my enquiries . . ."

In a July 30 letter to William Moore, president of the state of Pennsylvania, Atlee reported that the morning after the robbery "a number of the Inhabitants . . . were out in search of these fellows, . . . but I have not yet heard of their success." Be that as it may, neither Pile nor Buller appear to have been apprehended or prosecuted in connection with the hijackings.

Atlee said that "the destruction of public property, with design to distress our armies, seems the principal object with these villains though in the present case they have carried off a large quantity of valuable goods belonging to individuals,"

Jacob Miller told Atlee that the bandits said they had hijacked the wagons "in satisfaction for Fitz who was hanged. They said they would be revenged for him."

Earlier in the war, an outlaw named James Fitzpatrick—well-known as both "Captain Fitz" and "the Sandy Flash"—had committed many robberies in and around Chester County, some of them along the Lancaster Road. A deserter from the Continental Army, "Fitz" often robbed Continental soldiers and members of the Pennsylvania militia.

Fitz' last robbery occurred in August 1778 at the Chester County farmhouse of Robert McAfee. As chronicler John F. Watson reported in his 1887 Annals of Philadelphia, "Fitz entered the house . . . while they were at tea, armed with a rifle, a sword, and a case of pistols, saluting them as friends. Upon their saying they did not recognize him, he swore he would soon be better known as Captain Fitz, come to levy his dues on the cursed rebels."

Unfortunately for Fitz, McAfee soon after turned the tables on him and captured the bandit. Captain Fitz was hanged in Chester in September 1778.

Selected Bibliography

Colonial Records. Vol. VII. Harrisburg, PA: Theo. Fenn & Co., 1851.

Documents Relating to the Colonial History of the State of New Jersey, First Series. Vol. XXIX. Paterson, N.J.: The Call Printing and Publishing Company, 1917.

The Historical Magazine and Notes and Queries Concerning the Antiquities, History and Biography of America, Vol. 6. New York: Charles B. Richardson & Co., 1862

Historical Register: Notes and Queries, Historical and Genealogical Relating to Interior Pennsylvania, Number 1. Edited by William H. Egle. Harrisburg: William H. Egle, 1883-1884

Jeffries, Ewel. *A Short Biography of John Leeth with an Account of His Life Among the Indians.* Lancaster, Ohio: The Gazette Office, 1831. Reprint: The Burrows Brother Company, Cleveland, 1904.

Meginness, John F. *Otzinachson: A History of the West Branch Valley of the Susquehanna.* Williamsport, PA: Gazette and Bulletin Printing House, 1889.

Pennsylvania Archives, First Series. Vol. IV. Edited by Samuel Hazard. Philadelphia: Joseph Severns & Co., 1853.

———. Vol. V. Edited by Samuel Hazard. Philadelphia: Joseph Severns & Co., 1853.

———. Vol. VI. Edited by Samuel Hazard. Philadelphia: Joseph Severns & Co., 1853.

———. Vol. VII. Edited by Samuel Hazard. Philadelphia: Joseph Severns & Co., 1853.

———. Vol. IX. Edited by Samuel Hazard. Philadelphia: Joseph Severns & Co., 1854.

———. Vol. XII. Edited by Samuel Hazard. Philadelphia: Joseph Severns & Co., 1856.

The Pennsylvania Magazine of History and Biography. Vol. 29. Philadelphia: The Historical Society of Pennsylvania, 1905.

Thacher, James. *Military Journal during the American Revolutionary War from 1775 to 1783.* Boston: Richardson and Lord, 1823.

Swetland, Luke. *A Very Remarkable Narrative of Luke Swetland. Hartford, 1785.* (Reprinted by Garland Publishing Inc., New York, 1977.)

Wallace, Paul A. W. *Indian Paths of Pennsylvania.* Harrisburg: Pennsylvania Historical and Museum Commission, 1971.

About the Author

JOHN L. MOORE of Northumberland, Pa., writes non-fiction books about Colonial America and the early United States. They reflect a half century of research and travel throughout Pennsylvania and neighboring states.

A retired newspaperman, Moore said he employs a journalist's eye for detail and ear for quotes in order to write about 18th century people in a lively way. His books are based on letters, journals, memoirs and transcripts of interrogations, depositions and treaties.

He has participated in several archaeological excavations of Native American sites, including: the Village of Nain, Bethlehem, Pa.; the City Island project, Harrisburg, Pa. conducted by the Pennsylvania Historical and Museum Commission; and a Bloomsburg University dig near Nescopeck, Pa.

Moore's 46-year career included stints as a reporter for The Wall Street Journal, as managing editor of the (Sunbury, Pa.) Daily Item and as editor of the Eastern Pennsylvania Business Journal in Bethlehem, Pa.

His monthly history column appears in four Pennsylvania newspapers.

www.ingramcontent.com/pod-product-compliance
Lightning Source LLC
Chambersburg PA
CBHW020010050426
42450CB00005B/395